ASSESSING
INFORMATION NEEDS

ASSESSING INFORMATION NEEDS

Managing Transformative Library Services

Robert J. Grover, Roger C. Greer, and John Agada

LIBRARIES UNLIMITED

AN IMPRINT OF ABC-CLIO, LLC
Santa Barbara, California • Denver, Colorado • Oxford, England

Library of Congress Cataloging-in-Publication Data

Grover, Robert, 1942–
Assessing information needs : managing transformative library services / Robert J. Grover,
Roger C. Greer, and John Agada.
    p. cm.
Includes bibliographical references and index.
ISBN 978–1–59158–797–2 (alk. paper) — ISBN 978–1–59158–798–9 (ebook)
1. Library planning. 2. Public services (Libraries)—Planning. 3. Needs assessment.
4. Libraries and society. 5. Libraries and community. 6. Information services—Planning.
7. Information services—Use studies. 8. Information society. I. Greer, Roger C., 1928– II.
Agada, John. III. Title.
Z678.G75   2010
025.1—dc22   2010007504

ISBN: 978–1–59158–797–2
EISBN: 978–1–59158–798–9

14 13 12 11 10   1 2 3 4 5

This book is also available on the World Wide Web as an eBook.
Visit www.abc-clio.com for details.

Libraries Unlimited
An Imprint of ABC-CLIO, LLC

ABC-CLIO, LLC
130 Cremona Drive, P.O. Box 1911
Santa Barbara, California 93116-1911

This book is printed on acid-free paper ∞

Manufactured in the United States of America

CONTENTS

Acknowledgments   xi

1. Introduction   1
   Chapter Overview   1
   The Need for This Book   1
       Our Knowledge Society   2
       Managing for Change   2
       Knowing Your Clientele   3
   Audience   4
   Focus of the Book   4
   Overview of the Chapters   5
   Summary   6
   Reference   6

2. Libraries in Society—Past and Present   7
   Chapter Overview   7
   A Brief History of Library Services   7
       The Evolution of Library Services   8
       Emergence of a New Service Paradigm   9
   The Global Information Infrastructure   12
       The Role of Library and Information Professionals   13
       in the Information Infrastructure
   Current Changes in Society: Implications   16
       for Information Services
       Levels of User-Centered Services   17
       The Influence of Technology on Information Services   17

Summary   19
References   19
Suggested Reading on the History of Libraries   20

3. Knowledge Systems in Society   21
   Chapter Overview   21
      Definitions   21
   Community Information and Knowledge Infrastructure   23
      Social Knowledge and Information Services   27
      Elements of a Community Knowledge Infrastructure   28
   Formal and Informal Knowledge Systems and Resources   30
      The Relationship of Information Resources   30
         to Knowledge Systems
      Use as the Interface of Formal and Informal   31
         Knowledge Systems
   Implications for Assessing Information Needs   35
      and Customizing Information Services
   Summary   37
   References   37

4. The Theoretical Framework for Community Analysis   39
   Chapter Overview   39
   The Role of the Information Professional   39
      The Service Cycle   39
      The Diagnostic Process in Information Services   41
   The Definition of "Community Analysis"   43
      Evolution of the Greer Community Analysis Model   44
      Component Parts of the CARI Model   47
   Adapting to Community Change   48
      Community Change Requires Understanding the   49
         Past and Present
      Social Science Theories Are Necessary for Effective   50
         Analysis of a Community
   The Science of the Information Professions   51
      Information Psychology   52
      The Sociology of Information   53
   Summary   55
   References   56

5. Gathering Data for Decision-Making   57
   Chapter Overview   57
   Reader Studies   57
   Studies of Information Needs   58
      Environmental Scanning   60
      Community Analysis   63

Information Use Studies   64
The Use of Qualitative Research Methods and Intuition   65
When To Use Surveys—and When Not To   69
    Written Questionnaires   69
    Interviews   70
    Focus Groups   71
    When *Not* to Use Surveys   71
Using the Internet to Gather Community Information   72
Using Registration Data   72
Summary   72
References   73

6. The Information Needs of Individuals   75
    Chapter Overview   75
    Definition of Individuals   75
    Principles of Information Psychology   77
        Behavioral Processes of Information Psychology   77
        Theory Supporting Information Psychology   78
        The Environmental Context for Information Psychology   79
    Locating Data for Individuals   79
        Library Registration Files   79
        Census Data   80
        Using the Internet   82
    Summary   82
    References   83

7. Studying the Information Needs of Groups   85
    Chapter Overview   85
    Identifying Groups in a Community   85
        Sources of Information   87
        Examples of Groups   88
    What You Want to Know   92
    Implications for Library and Information Services   92
    Summary   93
    Reference   93

8. Studying the Information Needs of Agencies   95
    Chapter Overview   95
    Definition of Agencies   95
        Sources of Information   96
        Identifying Agencies   97
        Examples of Agencies   97
    Implications for Library and Information Services   102
    Summary   103
    References   103

9. Lifestyles   105
    Chapter Overview   105
    Definition of Lifestyles   105
    Exploring Culture in a Community   106
        History   107
        Values   108
        Customs   109
        Topographical Features   109
        Climate   110
        Leisure Activities   111
        Transportation and Traffic Patterns   112
        Communication   113
        Community-ness   115
        Economic Life   117
        Social Issues   118
    Summary   119
    References   120

10. Implementing a Community Analysis   121
    Chapter Overview   121
    Organizing to Gather Data   121
        Whom to Involve   122
        Organizing into Teams   122
    Community Analysis   123
        Collecting Data on Individuals, Groups, Agencies,   123
            and Lifestyles
        Library Resource Analysis   126
    What Do The Numbers Mean?   129
        Public Libraries   129
        School Libraries Media Centers   130
        Universities and Colleges   130
        Special Libraries   131
    Case Study   131
        Introduction to the Library District   132
        The Workshop   132
    Summary   135
    References   136

11. Extrapolating Meaning from Community Analysis Data   137
    Chapter Overview   137
    What the Data Tell Us   137
    Individuals   137
        Case Study Results   138
        What the Data Mean for Library Services   142

Groups   142
Agencies   148
  Agencies Case Study   149
  Implications for Information Services   150
Lifestyles   151
  Lifestyles Case Study   151
  Lifestyles Summary   154
Map Case Study   155
Registration File Case Study   157
Shelf List Data Case Study   157
A Review of the Community Analysis Process   159
  Authors' Note   160
Chapter Summary   160
References   160

12. Planning Information Services   163
Chapter Overview   163
Conceptualizing Information Services   163
  Functions of Information and Library Services   164
  Information and Library Services Functions Summary 173
  Levels of Service   173
Putting It All Together: The Role of the Professional   175
  Applying Data to Service Scenarios   175
Summary   179
References   180

13. Issues in Implementation   181
Chapter Overview   181
Today's Business Environment   181
  Leading Change   183
  Implementing a System for Change   184
Retaining Customers   186
The Challenge Ahead   186
References   187

Appendix A: Educational Attainment for the Six Communities   189

Appendix B: Brighton Businesses by Category   190

Appendix C: Brighton's History   191

Appendix D: Case Study Chronology   193

Appendix E: Case Study Survey Questions   195

Selected Bibliography   197

Index   201

ACKNOWLEDGMENTS

Many professionals, faculty, and students contributed to the ideas in this book. The basic concepts of this work have their roots in the work of four noteworthy giants in the field of systematic bibliography: Theodore Besterman, Verner Clapp, Ralph Shaw, and Jesse Shera. The development of the processes and their design and testing for a community analysis owes much to the contributions of Martha Hale, Dan O'Connor, Ann Douglas, Herbert Achleitner, Sally Patrick, and the late Natalia Greer (for her unwavering support for 37 years of effort in developing this methodology, and especially for the use of her library at Onondaga Hill, New York as a test site for this model).

As we wrote the manuscript for this book, we received strong support from leaders of the Rangeview Library District in Adams County Colorado. Pam Sandlian Smith, Director, became familiar with the CARI model while still a student in the Emporia State University School of Library and Information Management (SLIM) master's degree program in Denver. She embraced the client-centered approach to information services during her successful career and was quick to support our request to introduce the model in the Rangeview system.

We are grateful to Lynda Freas, formerly a professional colleague at Emporia State University and now Director of Family Services in the Rangeview District. Lynda was our first contact in the District, and she was very helpful introducing both ourselves and the community analysis process to her colleagues. We are especially grateful for her coordination of the community analysis and for her conscientious critique of our drafts.

The administrative team, branch heads, and staff members who participated in data-gathering for the case study were extremely helpful in providing
information that we could use to demonstrate how information from a needs
analysis can be converted into a successful plan for library and information
services.

Melody Bentfield, a student in the MLS program at Emporia State University SLIM in Colorado served valiantly as a collector and interpreter of data.
Her work laid the foundation for Chapter 11.

We are grateful to all who contributed to this book.

Bob Grover
Roger C. Greer
John Agada

CHAPTER 1

Introduction

CHAPTER OVERVIEW

This chapter introduces the book and the need it addresses. Librarians and other information professionals must manage their libraries in a time of great change, accompanied by the challenge of providing needed information services that are perceived as invaluable to the community they serve. This chapter describes the intended audience, amplifies the book's focus, and provides an overview of the chapters that follow.

THE NEED FOR THIS BOOK

Libraries and information agencies provide vital services to public and private organizations of all types, e.g., municipalities, corporations, schools, colleges and universities, museums, government agencies, and health agencies. In order to provide these necessary services in times of rapid and continuous change, librarians and information professionals must be able to make management decisions based on the changing needs of their constituencies—their actual needs, not their perceived needs. Furthermore, information professionals of all types cannot continue to provide those services that have been satisfactory in the past, especially providing access to collections of print and digitized information collections, without helping clientele to use the information effectively.

Information professionals must plan and implement services that transform individuals, groups, and agencies in their communities. Providing collections is only the starting point. To provide vital services, library and information professionals must be in constant touch with the changing needs of clientele and the social forces and technologies which influence them. The purpose of this book is to describe and demonstrate a model for systematically defining a community's needs and designing services to meet those needs.

Our Knowledge Society

We live in a *knowledge society*, a term coined by Peter Drucker in his 1959 book, *The Landmarks of Tomorrow* (Drucker 1995). Drucker explained the term as follows:

> In this society, knowledge is *the* primary resource for individuals and for the economy overall. Land, labor, and capital—the economist's traditional factors of production—do not disappear, but they become secondary. They can be obtained, and obtained easily, provided there is specialized knowledge. (Drucker 1995, 226)

In a knowledge society, information professionals, including librarians in all environments, play a prominent role because information professionals are expert at assisting in the collection, organization, and dissemination of information in any format. This capability is vital to the health of a knowledge society. The role of the information professional in the knowledge infrastructure is discussed further in Chapter 3.

Managing for Change

Another vital component of a knowledge society is the tendency for rapid and continuous change. Drucker emphasized the importance of change by stating "For managers, the dynamics of knowledge impose one clear imperative: every organization has to build the management of change into its very structure" (Drucker 1995, 79).

To manage change, Drucker has stated the requirements of organizations in the knowledge society: (1) Every organization must be ready to abandon everything it does, and (2) it must be devoted to creating the new. It must do this by:

1. Continuous improvement of everything it does;
2. Exploiting its knowledge and developing a new generation of applications;
3. Learning to innovate in a systematic way. (Drucker 1995, 79–80)

As vital components of our society, libraries and other information agencies must practice these methods of adroitly adapting to a changing environment.

An awareness of its surroundings is critical to every organization, and continuous monitoring of its constituencies assists in keeping an organization flexible, nimble, and vital. Therefore, analyzing one's community must be an ongoing process.

Although professionals may feel overwhelmed managing an information agency in this topsy-turvy world of change, they must rebuff the temptation to gasp "I'm too busy to conduct a community analysis! I just don't have time!" The response to that statement is this: You cannot afford NOT to do a continuous assessment of your community, regardless of the type of agency you manage. Libraries and other information agencies may be privately or publicly funded; in either case, information professionals must be able to deliver client-centered services. In order to discern the information needs of their clientele, information professionals must insist on an ongoing, systematic collection of data about its clientele. It helps to think of information agencies as businesses, and we can examine business practices to learn a rationale for customer service as well as methods for determining customer needs.

Knowing Your Clientele

While the analysis of users' needs has been in the library and information profession's rhetoric throughout its history, information professionals typically make management decisions and plan information services based on their experiences and intuition, what they **believe** to be the needs of their clientele. Furthermore, simply asking clientele to identify their needs is a fruitless task, because people cannot usually articulate the needs they have for information; however, information needs can be inferred from a study of what the clientele do. This book provides a proven model for collecting data to permit that inference.

The rationale for executing an information needs assessment is rooted in a philosophy of customer service. A focus on the customer is a fundamental concept of marketing literature, and this book provides both the rationale and techniques for identifying customer needs.

Conducting an information needs analysis requires the time of participating staff members, a valuable commodity in an organization that must justify its expenditures. How can we justify the time spent planning for a community analysis, providing the necessary continuing education for staff, spending the time to collect and analyze data, and the time-consuming process of weaving the data into the decision-making process? Is all of this worth the time, energy, and expense? How can librarians and other information professionals address these changing needs in an increasingly complex work environment? How can appropriate data be gathered in a systematic yet practical manner that can be translated into services? These are the major questions that are addressed in this book.

A certain proportion of a library's customer response is a given: "We can count on some of our business occurring just because we're a library" (about 25–35%, according to our studies). To increase that proportion is the goal of library managers, and it cannot be done without a community analysis.

AUDIENCE

This book is written for library and information practitioners in libraries, museums, and information centers in public and private agencies. When we use the term "information professionals," we refer to this intended audience. While the analysis of users' needs has been in the profession's literature since the writings of Melvil Dewey in the 1870s, information professionals typically make management decisions and plan information services based on their experiences and intuition. They "fly by the seat of their pants." This book provides the "why" (questions to be asked) and "how to" for professionals to organize and conduct effective data-gathering procedures on an ongoing basis. Once the data are gathered, we provide the know-how to analyze and use this information in planning services based on the data.

The book also is intended for students in degree programs of library and information science that prepare professionals for leadership positions in information agencies. As future information professionals build a theoretical framework for professional practice, they must also construct a client-centered philosophy for making professional decisions. This book provides these fundamental theories, philosophy, and practical applications, and it provides the social context with which new professionals may begin a career. The models and philosophy in this book will be pertinent and a useful reference throughout the student's career.

FOCUS OF THE BOOK

The focus of this book is "why" information professionals should customize services, as well as the "how to" of collecting data for decision-making. The rationale for gathering information needs assessment data is rooted in a philosophy of customer service. Without a philosophy grounded in the values of customer service, the processes of gathering data, analyzing it, and applying it are meaningless.

To address this focus on client-centered service, we apply social science (people-centered) theory to practice in libraries and other information agencies. This book describes the process of planning and implementing an information needs assessment in a community with reference to the "why," which is based on relevant social science and library/information science theories. The process of assessing information needs is a management process that results in customer-centered library and information services.

OVERVIEW OF THE CHAPTERS

Chapter 2 is a brief historical overview of libraries in society and the evolution of library and information services. The role of libraries in society is traced from that of standardized collecting, organizing, storing and disseminating of information (books), to that of customizing services to meet the needs of groups and individuals in a community.

In Chapter 3, "community" is defined and the role of libraries as part of the community knowledge infrastructure is explored. The role of community analysis is to analyze the components of that infrastructure as a management function. We describe how communities codify, document, and integrate their knowledge to meet society's needs. The focus is on the practical application of community analysis as a management function.

Chapter 4 introduces the Community Analysis Research Institute (CARI) model for community analysis and its development. This model, taught in more than one hundred workshops nationwide from 1975 to 2000 and applied in hundreds of libraries, identifies four variables that are essential to acquire a comprehensive understanding of the community and to determine its needs: individuals, groups, agencies, and lifestyles. In addition, the tension between change and preservation of the status quo is discussed, along with the need for reconceptualizing traditional values in the library profession.

Chapter 5 explores qualitative and quantitative research methods that can be used to assess community information needs. The literature of pertinent library and information user needs is reviewed, and the rationale for using informal and qualitative data-gathering methods is outlined.

Chapter 6 explains how to collect data about individuals who reside in a community, one of the variables in the CARI model. The chapter provides an overview of principles associated with information psychology, and sources of information about individuals in a community are suggested.

In Chapter 7, "groups" is defined with examples, and sources of community information about groups are explored and discussed. One of the characteristics of group needs is the specificity or certainty of their information needs, which can easily be identified.

Chapter 8 defines "agencies," with examples, and their role in the community. Methods for gathering information about agencies are investigated. Agencies exist because there is a need for their services by the community. The information agency should be aware of this need and work to enhance it.

"Lifestyles" is defined in Chapter 9, and sources of information for determining the culture of a community are discussed. Examining lifestyles provides a look into the community as reflected in the knowledge infrastructure that enlivens the culture.

Chapter 10 provides examples for using the four perspectives in a community with applications to public, school, academic, and special libraries. The process of converting data into decisions is described, with examples.

Chapter 11 explains what the data mean and how they can be used to customize new or existing services in libraries and information agencies. A case study is analyzed with implications for information services. Much of the data in this chapter are included in the Appendix.

Chapter 12 discusses information services and applies the results of the Chapter 11 case study to demonstrate the application of data attained from a community analysis.

Chapter 13 summarizes the rationale for the community analysis process and draws upon business literature. Leaders of libraries and information agencies must continuously monitor their communities in order to provide vital services.

SUMMARY

Knowing an organization's community enables library and information professionals to prioritize a community's information needs and design services to address those needs. This book provides the rationale for community analysis, presents a model for gathering community data, and explains a process for analyzing data and applying it to the management of an information agency. The analysis part distinguishes the professional library personnel from clerical and housekeeping functions; it enables librarians to demonstrate their professional knowledge to their community by diagnosing their information needs and designing those services that transform clientele.

REFERENCE

Drucker, Peter F. 1995. *Managing in a time of great change.* New York: Truman Talley Books/Dutton.

CHAPTER 2

Libraries in Society—Past and Present

CHAPTER OVERVIEW

This chapter provides an overview of the development of library services from the archival storage of documents to the customization of information services to meet user needs. We also examine the evolution of the library and information professions to their current state in order to understand the context for conducting an analysis of a user community. The global information infrastructure is discussed, as well as the role of library and information professionals as dynamic leaders in the further development of the infrastructure. The impact of technology on information transfer and the changing role of information professionals are addressed, along with suggestions for remaining current on technology trends.

A BRIEF HISTORY OF LIBRARY SERVICES

This brief history and discussion of libraries is adapted from Greer, Grover, and Fowler (2007). The history of libraries can be traced back five thousand years, and ancient libraries can be categorized into four groups: (1) government, (2) religious, (3) commercial, and (4) private or family libraries.

- Government libraries collected the treaties, legislation, and genealogy of the royal family, lines of succession, and other recorded documents pertinent to governance in a variety of formats, e.g., clay tablets, papyrus scrolls, and parchment. The information sources were arranged physically by subjects, often in different rooms. The major role of the librarian was to store and preserve as well as catalog or arrange the items for retrieval. We can generalize that a civilization progressed when it developed a written language and kept archives of their past. Primitive societies that did not have archives of their past could not advance beyond the knowledge that could be remembered, and they tended not to advance to a sophisticated state.

- Religious libraries were formed for the education of the clergy. The creed of the religion, the beliefs, sacred writings, and rituals of the religion or sect were recorded and stored.
- Commercial libraries stored and organized the records of commerce, including bills of lading and business papers, commercial agreements, and other records of various kinds.
- Private and family libraries archived the private papers, records of property holdings, and the relationships between the family and rulers or government of the day.

The function of libraries as archives dominated their use until the later years of the nineteenth century. Archives were perceived as a collection of valuable and pertinent knowledge that required maintenance but did not require assistance to the library's users. The evolution of library and information services is described below. Additional information on the history of libraries can be found in the bibliography at the end of this chapter.

The Evolution of Library Services

Public libraries first developed by emphasizing their archival role. The next service to emerge was the educational role. The first instance of government support for libraries occurred when New York governor Dewitt Clinton established libraries in New York state school districts in the 1830s. During the 1850s, the first public library for the common person was established in Boston. Following the mission of the earlier "mechanics" and "mercantile" libraries, the Boston Public Library fulfilled the educational role as well as the cultural role; the objective of the mechanics and mercantile libraries of the industrial revolution was to enable factory workers to educate themselves in preparation for positions as middle managers in the factories.

With the development of the industrial revolution due in some measure to the production of steam power, manufacturers could expand production. Companies grew, and middle managers were needed. Community leaders wanted to encourage self-education, and for that purpose, libraries needed to acquire the best books—the cultural function of libraries. Although collecting for the purpose of educating clientele and enhancing the culture of library patrons, librarians continued to place a high value on the collection itself, so that the archival function was maintained, i.e., books were considered treasures that must be preserved.

Concurrent with these developments in the mid-1800s was the emergence of the social science disciplines. The population in the United States was growing, as were the social problems: increased crime, changing family relationships, abandoned children, and public health issues. Professionals were needed to teach, to manage schools, hospitals and prisons, and to resolve other emerging social problems. This demand for professional services fostered the development of the disciplines and professions to address these social problems. Originally, it was the wealthier classes who had the benefit of higher education, including the clergy. When the privileged classes discovered the need for methods to manage social problems, the professions grew, and libraries were needed to support them.

Special libraries gradually developed following the American Civil War because industry needed new products, and libraries supported innovation and the creation of new products. This is an example, then, of libraries supporting the research function, the creation of new knowledge.

The information function began with the urging of Melvil Dewey and Samuel S. Green, who encouraged assertive librarians to work with clientele to help them use libraries and their resources. The information function became more prevalent with the increasing use of computers; it is now a dominant function of information agencies.

Recreational reading as a library service was frowned upon until the beginning of the twentieth century. The practice came into its own with the emergence of the paperback book industry in the 1930s, and became even more widespread after World War II. Recreational reading has evolved to encompass a variety of recreational resources in such formats as CDs, DVDs, games, and Internet resources.

In the beginning, and still today, we see an incremental increase in different services. Initially, service was passive and the book was a treasure. Over time, passive service evolved into reactive service, whereby librarians responded to requests for information, which brought us to Dewey and Green. Assertive service is more recent, a result of progress in the library profession and the emergence of a service paradigm, as discussed below.

Emergence of a New Service Paradigm

As described above, the 1880s saw the beginning of a paradigm shift in the field of library science, the emergence of service. That shift is still in progress, as evidenced in the curricula of library and information science programs, some of which reflect that change.

Two important events occurred during that decade, both initiated by Melvil Dewey, then the Director of Libraries of Columbia University. The first event, in 1886, was the initiation of a program of studies at the undergraduate level, which Dewey called Library Economy. The focus of this program was consistent with the concepts commonly held in the profession, namely that the proper function of the library staff was the orderly management of the library and its collections.

The second event was less striking at the time, but eventually gained significance as the founding of an academic library education program. This event was the establishment of a formal reference service in the Columbia University libraries. To implement this service, Dewey employed twin brothers to staff a reference desk full time. That he had committed some of the library's resources for the express purpose of assisting library users in their quest for information was a profound departure from traditional library management. Suddenly, the library user was brought into the service paradigm. Though the program at Columbia University was successfully imitated by large university and municipal libraries, the 100th anniversary of this event passed in the 1980s with minimal acknowledgement by the library profession. This event marked the beginning of a shift from focus on book collections to focus on services to clientele.

Until the later part of the nineteenth century, the dominant paradigm of librarianship was preoccupation with collection development and the acquisition of works by the best authors in every field. In addition, the orderly management of the library staff and facility was paramount. Classification and bibliography were important elements of this paradigm. Missing was a concern for the library user. Some papers presented at the first American Library Association (ALA) conference in 1876 encouraged staff to offer help to library patrons. However, it was not until Dewey's decision to staff the reference desk that the concept of service was incorporated as a legitimate function of a library. Incidentally, a proper intellectual goal for a librarian at this time was to be known as a "bookman" who could identify important works in any field and recite them from memory.

The implementation of Dewey's concept of reference service was slow. By the 1950s, the concepts of reference service and reader's service were a fundamental part of large libraries, but outside of the large metropolitan and university libraries, these services generally were not found.

Library education evolved to the fifth-year graduate degree in the 1930s and to a fifth-year master's degree in 1950. The outcome labels changed, but the curricula remained reasonably consistent with Dewey's program of Library Economy, except for the addition of children's literature and some technology courses. The educational programs reflected the book-focused paradigm of the profession, and the concept of service was limited. Courses concentrated on collections and bibliographic control of materials. These courses were essentially "how to" courses with an emphasis on the memorization of reference titles and their characteristics, publishing houses, book jobbers, reviewing media, and the elements of the U.S. national bibliography. This was typical of MLS curricula at that time. Some schools prided themselves on their progressiveness by adding technology courses, especially courses on audiovisual equipment and materials. In all of this, the dominant paradigm remained undisturbed by Dewey's embrace of the library user.

In 1968, Roger Greer, dean of the School of Library Science at Syracuse University, led the faculty there in development of a new Ph.D. program. He and the faculty wanted a curriculum heavily weighted with research methods and statistics courses, but which gave some attention to the theories associated with communication and social psychology. When they chose a name for this program, they found that the Electrical Engineering Department had preempted the title of "information science." They did not want to call it "library science" nor suggest its focus was library management; they opted instead for the title "Ph.D. in Information Transfer." The term "information transfer" was explored over the ensuing decade, and the faculty at University of Southern California (USC), under the leadership of Greer, developed in 1980 a curriculum focused on the concept of information transfer.

During the curriculum discussions at USC, several basic principles were articulated and adopted as guides. These basic principles were:

- Information science is an academic discipline of the social sciences, and library and information management are the applied professions supported by the theories developed through research within this discipline.
- The program must follow normal graduate level curricula, beginning with broad theoretical courses and progressing to the specific, i.e., first courses would concentrate on theory. Subsequent courses would look at the application of theory to practice.
- Theory courses would be anchored in several disciplines of the social sciences, particularly sociology, psychology, and management.
- Instead of focusing on books, e.g., children's literature, all courses would concentrate on the processes of information transfer within specific groups of people and various fields and disciplines. This meant that paradigmatic constraints, communication patterns, and information sources were to be examined with each group.
- Techniques and the process of needs assessment were to be the core of each area of information transfer.
- It was recognized that new technologies were important parts of the profession and must be studied as a means of enhancing the flow of information, not as ends in themselves.

This curriculum was launched at the University of Southern California in 1980 and implemented at Emporia State University in 1983 through the leadership of Bob Grover and Herbert Achleitner. While it has since been modified and updated with changing technologies, it is a reflection of the client-centered paradigm first implemented by Melvil Dewey. Studying the needs of library users and special population groups has become a relatively common activity for information professionals today.

THE GLOBAL INFORMATION INFRASTRUCTURE

An information professional must understand the role of libraries and other information agencies in the global information infrastructure to understand fully the big picture of information transfer and the role of information agencies. Greer, Grover, and Fowler (2007, 98) propose the following definition of "information infrastructure":

> The information infrastructure is a **global** network of **people, organizations, agencies, policies, processes, and technologies** organized in a loosely coordinated system to enhance the creation, production, dissemination, organization, storage, retrieval, and preservation of information and knowledge for people. The primary objective of this network is the diffusion of knowledge for a society.

Technology is frequently the focus when information infrastructure is discussed. Nevertheless, we want to focus not on technology, but on the users and human element of the information infrastructure. The core of the information professions must be a focus on people as users of information, and the secondary focus must be on the design of organizations and services to deliver the information needed by those users. Libraries are but one element of the information infrastructure. Managing a library or database is a significant but specific activity. Other information professions are defined by the kinds of information systems they manage within the information infrastructure, e.g., archives, museums, networks, web sites, and records in a variety of formats. Technologies will change, but how people process information is important—the most significant concern of the information professions. Some of the current Internet search engines may provide people with the opportunity to find their own information, but information professionals give a value-added component to save searchers time.

Because of the Internet, we want to emphasize the **global** nature of the infrastructure. The information infrastructure of the world is a vast system that includes news organizations, universities, corporate researchers, satellite transmission systems, think tanks, newspapers and magazines, radio and television stations and networks, government agencies, publishers, libraries, schools, and other organizations and agencies engaged in research and mass distribution of information and knowledge. In a knowledge society, software producers and professionals are also a part of this infrastructure. The network is so vast that it employs a sizeable segment of the adult population. This infrastructure extends much beyond the technology itself and the policies, agencies, and processes that govern its use.

Similarly, individual communities have an information infrastructure, i.e., the people, organizations, agencies, policies, processes, and technologies organized in a system to enhance the transfer of information to members of that community. Public, university, school, and special librarians should take responsibility for determining the players in their communities and how each can be advanced by an effective information system. The library should be a leader in the development of a community information infrastructure for any environment, municipality, school, college or university, law firm, health facility, public agency, or private sector enterprise. This community information infrastructure is explored further in Chapter 3.

Since we have identified the major elements of the information infrastructure, we will begin exploring how library and information professionals can contribute to the information infrastructure through their work in libraries and other information agencies.

The Role of Library and Information Professionals in the Information Infrastructure

Library and information professionals have a vital role in the development and operation of the global information infrastructure. A library or other information agency is no longer an isolated agency within a community, a school, a corporation, or a government agency. It has been brought into a global network by the Internet. As more individuals, groups, and agencies join that network, the more complex it becomes, and the more information professionals are needed to make sense of the information and systems that comprise the Internet.

Information professionals with a Master of Library Science degree (or its equivalent) can appropriately organize and manage any of the agencies that are in the information infrastructure. The development and articulation of this information infrastructure is the intellectual contribution that information professionals should be making to academia. Currently, discussions about the information infrastructure are often limited to discussions of the Internet, and so narrow in their scope that it seems that discussions of bibliographic control have deteriorated into storage and retrieval issues. When the discussion conceptualizes the issue to only a fragment of the whole, much is lost.

The information transfer model shown in Figure 2.1 enables library and information professionals to think of the ways they can become actively involved in the information transfer process regardless of the technology that is employed. It is a way of thinking about the library and information profession (Greer, Grover, and Fowler 2007, 124–125).

Figure 2.1   The Information Transfer Cycle.

Creation
↓
Recording
↓
Mass production
↓
Organization
↓
Dissemination
↓
Bibliographic control
↓
Diffusion
↓
Organization by discipline
↓
Utilization
↓
Preservation

Each of the categories of the information transfer model is listed below with suggestions for an information professional's involvement.

- **Knowledge creation and recording.** Information professionals can assist researchers by helping them to identify keys to the research literature in the field—indexes, bibliographies, catalogs, and leading researchers—and identifying special or subject area encyclopedias, textbooks, and authoritative web sites which provide an overview of the field of study if the researcher is engaging in interdisciplinary research.
- **Mass production of information.** Information professionals can provide leadership in the work that is done in the publishing, broadcasting, and web mastery fields.
- **Dissemination of information.** Information professionals have traditionally excelled in this portion of the information transfer process by acquiring, organizing, and circulating information and knowledge, primarily in the form of periodicals and books. With the many formats available today, the role of information professionals has expanded to include expertise in the newer media for disseminating information, including the Internet.

- **Bibliographic control.** Librarians are heavily engaged in the cataloging and classification of knowledge and information. The organization of books, periodicals, videos, compact discs, and various forms of computer-stored information is a vital role of information professionals. This organization includes the application of special vocabularies and unique organizational schemes for subject fields.
- **Diffusion of knowledge.** Librarians throughout history have assisted clients who were engaged in learning. With the paradigm shift from the archival role to diffusion (see the earlier discussion), information professionals were thrust into responsible roles in the information transfer process. The role of librarians in public libraries, schools, universities, colleges is more important than ever due to the growing number of people returning for continuing education, to prepare for a new occupation, or to learn at a distance. The role of the librarian is to help the learner locate appropriate resources in various formats and, through knowledge of the information transfer process, help clients understand the information they encounter. With the proliferation of information now available, it is incumbent upon information professionals to go beyond dissemination to diffusion, helping users understand the new knowledge in a field and helping them make meaning of the research. As a result, librarians and other information professionals are engaging in information skills instruction, also known as "bibliographic instruction." Professional literature documents the increasing importance of the information professional's role as a teacher, someone actively engaged in the diffusion of new knowledge.
- **Organization by subject discipline.** When information professionals are aware of the needs, vocabulary, and values of constituent groups, unique terms and organization schemes can be constructed and implemented for those groups. The organization of resources, then, is customized for each discipline, profession, or other group.
- **Information utilization.** All information professionals should be engaged in helping individuals and groups to use information effectively, a result of effectively diffusing information and knowledge. Contemporary society requires that people stay current in their use of information.
- **Preservation of information.** All information agencies and information professionals should be engaged in the evaluation of information and the preservation of the information, regardless of format, which has lasting value for the organization and the clientele of that organization. Information professionals must be aware of the information needs of clientele both now and in the future. Information professionals should assess the value of a given document (either print

or electronic) to determine its relevance to the agency mission and its potential for providing a valuable artifact, vital content, or informative context. To make an effective decision, the information professional must collaborate with information users and agency decision makers to develop policies and procedures for either the effective preservation or the discarding of information packages.

In all of these roles, information professionals must count on the needs of their clientele. The information professional must diagnose the information needs of individuals and assess the needs of a community in order to create and manage libraries and information systems for the delivery of needed information services. This work is challenging because of the constant change we experience in society today.

CURRENT CHANGES IN SOCIETY: IMPLICATIONS FOR INFORMATION SERVICES

Professions are anchored in society. The function of professions in society is to provide customized services employing specialized knowledge in an ethical manner. To be effective, a profession must reflect the current thought, activity, and social dynamic of the parent society. While there are many characteristics one may choose to describe the social environment at the beginning of the twenty-first century, perhaps the most compelling is the concept of change.

Change is the byproduct of many variables evolving and interacting with each other. A list of some of these variables can lead us to a broader understanding of the concept of change. Perhaps the dominant variable among the developed societies of the world is the new technologies that appear at an unprecedented rate. Each new technology seeks to improve our ability to manage our daily occupational and domestic routines. Furthermore, the addition of a new technology is not necessarily a replacement for an existing tool, but often is merely an additional device or methodology. A person wishing to attend to a task or engage in an activity has more options in choice of tools or techniques to employ. With the addition of yet more options comes increased complexity.

New technologies lead to greater complexity because of the things that can be accomplished now which were impossible in the past. Astonishing developments in space exploration are compelling examples of this change. Advances in medical technologies and techniques have increased longevity. New drugs designed to pinpoint and ameliorate the effects of illness, from deadly cancer to simple headaches, are contributing to the general expansion of the human race. Increased population combined with enhanced communication and transportation technologies has profoundly contributed to the reality of a global economy.

More people, and more social complexity through enhanced communication and transportation, necessarily provoke a deluge of information to provide the glue necessary for the maintenance of a dynamic society. All of these developments contribute to an accelerated rate of change influencing every individual, organization, community, society, and culture in the world. Understanding the existence of this explosion of change is essential for professions and for professionals seeking means of satisfying individual and group needs

As noted above, the "people paradigm" replaces the focus on collection of information with a focus on people. This is a relatively simple concept, but one that is often overlooked in professional practice. To illustrate the impact of a user-centered professional library and information service, we present below a model for planning levels of service.

Levels of User-Centered Services

A model for outlining levels of service was first introduced by Greer and Hale (1982) and uses the following terms:

- *Passive level of service*, which provides the resources (books, journals, computer software, etc.) for use with no help from the professional staff.
- *Reactive level of service*, which provides professional assistance when the user requests help.
- *Assertive level of service*, which anticipates the needs of clientele based upon the results of a systematic community analysis.

These levels of service can be applied to the various information services provided in any library or information center. Types of services are discussed later in Chapter 12 of this book, "Planning Information Services."

The Influence of Technology on Information Services

Technology has changed nearly every aspect of our lives, especially our communication patterns. Cell phones permeate society; it is estimated that 87 percent of the population in the United States own cell phones; and 94 percent of Americans under the age of 45 own cell phones (Tickets.com 2009). Cell phones are ubiquitous and have become a nuisance as people drive cars, walk down busy streets, and sit in public places talking on them. In addition to their use for real-time communication between individuals, cell phones can also transmit text messages, e-mail, music, and news to cell phone users.

The Internet is now available on multi-dimensional cell phones as well as on portable computers of all types: laptops, handhelds, and tablet computers.

As computers become smaller, more powerful, and possess greater storage capacity, their use for transferring information must be taken in to account as library and information professionals evaluate and plan library and information services.

Available over the Internet and readily accessible to growing numbers in society are wikis, blogs, and web sites. These self-published electronic documents must be acknowledged by library and information professionals and integrated into information service. Additionally, information professionals must instruct information users on evaluating these newer forms of information, along with the more traditional electronic and paper resources.

Challenges of Keeping Current with Technology

The enormous impact of technology on the information transfer process holds implications for the roles of library and information professionals, who are engaged in all phases of the information transfer process as never before. However, the changes driven by technology require information professionals to be alert to emerging trends in technology. But how can that be done? Some suggestions follow.

Staying current is like herding cats; it is very difficult to feel that you are making any real progress. The best solution is to be active in an appropriate professional organization that addresses your segment of the library and information profession. The larger professional organizations, such as the American Library Association (ALA), the Special Libraries Association (SLA), the American Society for Information Science and Technology (ASIST), and some other more specialized associations (the Medical Library Association, the American Association of Law Libraries, and the Society of American Archivists) have state or regional chapters. Attendance at state, regional, and national conferences is the best way to network and stay current on trends and technology applications in the field.

Networking is one key to staying current. The professional colleagues you meet at professional conferences can be valuable sources of help for issues that arise on the job. Since many professional positions are in small agencies, professional collegiality may be scant or non-existent in your local area; however, professional networks can be very effective thanks to e-mail and telephone communication. Membership in national, regional, and/or state organizations is vital to one's professional growth.

In addition to conferences, professional organizations include, with membership, subscription to professional journals and newsletters, many of which are electronic and easily accessible. These professional publications provide update articles, news of upcoming professional meetings and workshops, and the names of leaders in the field, more potential members of your network. Professional conferences also provide the opportunity for hands-on learning opportunities with new technologies and processes. Vendors provide workshops at conferences, and exhibit areas enable the conference goer to view and try out new technologies and resources. Salespeople are readily available to share the benefits of their products (the negative points you'll need to discover on your own, another value of a professional network). Sales personnel can be very helpful in our efforts to be current, but one must remember that their primary job is to sell their products.

In addition to professional organizations, the Coalition for Networked Information (CNI) is "an organization dedicated to supporting the transformative promise of networked information technology for the advancement of scholarly communication and the enrichment of intellectual productivity." (web site) Founded in 1990, CNI is comprised of 200 institutions representing higher education, publishing, network and telecommunications, information technology, and libraries and library organizations. CNI hosts a variety of networked information projects to help information professionals to stay current.

Classes are available face-to-face in many communities, and distance learning opportunities are readily available for those seeking updates. Still another approach is to form study groups among colleagues to share ideas, read books, consult web sites, participate in webinars, and discuss trends informally. Informal discussion groups can be formed within an agency or among professionals who are geographically nearby. With the availability of e-mail and social networks, list discussions and exchanges on such networking sites as Facebook enable professionals to exchange ideas unrestricted by geographical proximity.

Regardless of the format or channel of communication, information professionals MUST stay current in order to provide effective information services using current technologies.

SUMMARY

This chapter has traced the history of libraries, information services, and library science education to provide the reader a context for considering information services. The global information infrastructure is described, as well as the role of library and information professionals as leaders in the further development of that infrastructure. The impact of technology on information transfer, and the changing role of information professionals are addressed. Strategies are suggested for remaining current in a rapidly changing, technological society to keep abreast of our changing society and changing needs of library and information clientele.

REFERENCES

"About CNI." Coalition for Networked Information web site. http://www.cni.org/organization.html (accessed November 19, 2007).

Greer, Roger C., Robert J. Grover and Susan G. Fowler. 2007. *Introduction to the library and information professions.* Westport, CN and London: Libraries Unlimited.

Greer, Roger C. and Martha L. Hale. 1982. "The community analysis process." In *Public librarianship, a reader,* ed. Jane Robbins-Carter, 358–366. Littleton, CO.: Libraries Unlimited.

Tickets.com. Mobile trends: Americans' cell phone ownership statistics. September 3, 2009. http://ticketsdotcom.blogspot.com/search/label/mobile%20trends. Accessed September 21, 2009.

SUGGESTED READING ON THE HISTORY OF LIBRARIES

Armour, Richard Willard. 1976. *The happy bookers: a playful history of librarians and their world from the stone age to the distant future.* New York: McGraw-Hill.

Battles, Matthew. 2003. *Library: an unquiet history.* New York: W.W. Norton.

Casson, Lionel. 2001. *Libraries in the ancient world.* New Haven: Yale University Press.

Harris, Michael H. 1995. *History of libraries in the western world.* 4th ed. Metuchen, NJ & London: Scarecrow Press.

Lerner, Frederick Andrew. 1999. *Libraries through the ages.* New York: Continuum.

Richardson, John V. 1982. *The spirit of inquiry: the Graduate Library School at Chicago, 1921–51.* Chicago: American Library Association.

Shera, Jesse Hauk. 1965. *Foundations of the public library; the origins of the public library movement in New England, 1629–1885.* Hamden, CT: Shoe String Press.

———. 1965. *Libraries and the organization of knowledge.* Hamden, CT: Archon Books.

———. 1973. *Knowing books and men; knowing computers, too.* Littleton, CO: Libraries Unlimited.

Wiegand, Wayne A. 1996. *Irrepressible reformer: a biography of Melvil Dewey.* Chicago: American Library Association.

CHAPTER 3

Knowledge Systems in Society

CHAPTER OVERVIEW

This chapter explores knowledge systems in society and the role of libraries and information agencies as knowledge sources and agents for the dissemination and diffusion of knowledge. After defining key terms, we outline the elements of a community knowledge infrastructure and relate it to the information infrastructure. In so doing, we examine formal and informal knowledge systems with implications for library and information agencies. Finally, we discuss the rationale for a community information needs analysis as a means for integrating a library or other information agency into its community knowledge system.

Definitions

People often use the terms *information* and *knowledge* interchangeably. We do not. We define **information** using Cleveland's (1985) definition as organized data, which are the rough materials from which information and knowledge are formed, i.e., undigested observations, or "unvarnished facts," as Cleveland calls them. For example, researchers collect data from interviews, observations, surveys, and other means in order to analyze it for research purposes. We are bombarded with data all the time. To make sense of it, data must be selected, organized, and synthesized. Data may take the form of words, numbers, or visual images. By themselves, data make no sense. Given connections or context, data can form information.

Knowledge, according to Cleveland (1985, 22), " ... is organized information, internalized by me, integrated with everything else I know from experience or study or intuition, and therefore useful in guiding my life and work." This concept is generally accepted in the current knowledge management (KM) literature, as explained by Mason (2007, 23–24):

> One generally imagines a flow to this hierarchy [data/information/ knowledge], with 'raw' data that are arranged in ways that are meaningful in order to produce information, and then this information is consolidated into coherent frameworks to form knowledge.

The noise of a distant train's whistle, a passing car, conversation in the next room, the sound of a furnace or air conditioner, or the television in the background as we read all give us data or information that we may reject or do not retain or remember. When we watch the television news or read a newspaper, we remember only a small percentage of what we read, view, or listen to. That which we remember or incorporate in to our memory bank becomes knowledge. In other words, information that is processed, selected, and synthesized by a human becomes knowledge.

Information is communicated using various kinds of symbols—numerals, pictures, and words—but knowledge is an understanding of information that occurs because people have provided a context and meaning for the information. Information is transmitted, but the end result is a more comprehensive knowledge, a deeper understanding of phenomena. In summary, information constitutes knowledge when accumulated, organized, and given meaning by an individual or group.

In addition to **personal or individual knowledge**, we must recognize that society has acceptable knowledge that we call **social knowledge**. As with personal knowledge, social knowledge requires the selection, analysis, and synthesis of information in order to be accepted as knowledge.

Wilson (1977, 3–4) recognized that one cannot easily conceptualize social knowledge and private or individual knowledge.

> The public stock of knowledge is not simply the sum of what is known by the separate individuals in the world; it is at once more and less than that. It is less, simply because much of what individuals know has not been and never will be, made public. It is more, because much of what is known may be known *to* no one at all. A discovery made a hundred years ago, and preserved in the published records of inquiry, may still be a part of what is known about the world, even though no one now alive has ever examined the records in which it is preserved.

Social knowledge is knowledge that has been accepted by recognized experts for inclusion in a given body of knowledge. For example, history professors are the experts who conduct research and use a system of peer review to determine if newly conducted historical research used conventional and acceptable methods with results consistent with the dominant paradigm of their discipline. Print and broadcast journalists and bloggers produce current information that, when reviewed by acknowledged experts, can become social knowledge.

A knowledge system is integral to the culture of a community, defining how its members live their lives based on their understanding of themselves and their environment and how they share knowledge with each other. The infrastructure is the vehicle, the set of tools or agents, by which the culture builds the connections between knowledge and information that must be created, packaged, and used. Each society has its own system, a **knowledge infrastructure**. In the sections that follow, we describe the process by which new information becomes social knowledge and the infrastructure that supports the creation, diffusion, and use of knowledge in a community.

COMMUNITY INFORMATION AND KNOWLEDGE INFRASTRUCTURE

Understanding a community knowledge system becomes easier when we first identify the elements of the information transfer process: how information and knowledge are created, recorded, disseminated, and used. A model for the information transfer process was created by Greer (Greer, Grover, and Fowler 2007), and was outlined in Figure 2.1. This model can also be outlined with these questions posed by Greer and adapted to address knowledge transfer:

1. What are the patterns of information and knowledge creation? How is new knowledge created? What are the accepted research methods?

2. What are the systems for recording new information and knowledge? As research is conducted and new information is created, how is it recorded? What technologies are used in the recording process?

3. What are the mechanisms for the mass production of information and knowledge? After research is completed, how is this research packaged for distribution to a large audience? What are the accepted presses for publishing? Which electronic media are used?

4. What varieties of systems are employed in the dissemination of new information and knowledge? When the new information or knowledge has been packaged for mass distribution, what are the professional associations, professional conferences, publishers, conferences, mass media, and web sites used to distribute the new knowledge?

5. What systems for bibliographic control of the records are being produced in society? What are the bibliographies, databases,

webographies, indexes, and other organizing tools which organize knowledge in this area and make it available to audiences?

6. What is the paradigmatic structure for the organization of knowledge by subject fields? Within this specialty area, how does this knowledge fit into the discipline or profession? What special terms are used to organize and retrieve this knowledge?

7. What are the patterns of diffusion of knowledge? How and through what social organizations is this new knowledge likely to be taught to others? What are the leading universities or other social agencies which specialize in passing on new knowledge in the field?

8. How have disciplines and other groups in society developed information and knowledge organization schemes using their unique vocabulary?

9. How is new knowledge used in society? What are likely user groups who would put this new knowledge to use?

10. What systems exist for the preservation of knowledge? Which agencies are likely to preserve this knowledge? What means would be used to maintain the knowledge? (Adapted from Greer, Grover, and Fowler 2007, 49)

Responses to these questions provide a comprehensive understanding of how information and knowledge are created and used. When information is created, recorded, disseminated, and accepted by an individual or group, it becomes knowledge, individual or social. Furthermore, the responses to these ten questions provide a framework for understanding the breadth and depth of the information and knowledge infrastructure of a community.

While the above questions show the complexity of our information and knowledge infrastructure, a more concise definition has been offered by the authors, as discussed in Chapter 2. We repeat it here for further discussion:

The information infrastructure is a **global** network of **people, organizations, agencies, policies, processes, and technologies** organized in a loosely coordinated system to enhance the creation, production, dissemination, organization, storage, retrieval, and preservation of information and knowledge for people. The primary objective of this network is the diffusion of knowledge for a society. (Greer, Grover, and Fowler 2007, 98)

When people attain bits of knowledge that complement their existing knowledge, they expand their personal knowledge; therefore, the knowledge infrastructure enables individuals and groups to draw from social knowledge to build personal knowledge.

We define the knowledge infrastructure as those institutions and agents that acquire, store, and diffuse bodies of knowledge. Examples of these institutions and agencies are schools, universities, churches, political parties, and professionals of various kinds. A professional is an individual who has acquired a defined and unique body of knowledge and applies that knowledge in society, usually for the individual's financial gain. The knowledge infrastructure deals with only that information that has been accepted by a societal group as social knowledge, or by an individual as personal knowledge. Any individual or organization that engages in training or education is part of the knowledge infrastructure.

To state it another way, knowledge is the product of an information infrastructure when that information is integrated into an individual's or group's knowledge system. Librarians who assist individuals and groups in their learning do so by identifying gaps in the knowledge base of their clienetele and by identifying resources to fill those gaps. In other words, libraries and other information agencies and their staffs help people solve their problems. Libraries, information centers, archives, and museums are all significant parts of the knowledge infrastructure.

Information resources and information agencies can fill a knowlege gap. So can schools and institutions of higher education, which are responsible for transferring knowledge of a community from one individual to another, from one group to another, and from one generation to another.

A community knowledge system or infrastructure consists of four basic elements:

1. **Knowledge that has been generated by society**, based on both experience and research. This includes social and cultural knowledge; cultural knowledge includes the values, norms, rules of conduct, and knowledge accepted as truth in the culture. A society or community develops over time a substantial body of knowledge which may be both recorded and oral. Some of this knowledge may be inert until activated in an information system. An example is the knowledge of gardening, which can be handed down from parent to child, read about in books, acquired through reading horticulture periodicals, or learned in a class or during a conversation with a friend who is an experienced gardener. The knowledge exists and may be recorded in a variety of formats or passed on orally. It can be printed or recorded as a video or stored in a database.

   Books and other recorded knowledge are extractions from the collection of social knowledge in a field of study. A person who reads the book may extract bits of knowledge and make sense of it. For example, medical students extract knowledge from medical school classes and books to form their professional knowldedge. Their skills and knowledge related to medicine are a fraction of the knowledge in their minds. Books can represent neither all knowledge on a topic nor all knowledge in a mind. All recorded social knowledge is but a fraction of the knowledge available to be known.

2. **Practical skills or tools**, resources used to enact a body of knowledge. Knowledge itself is inert until an individual or group which possesses that knowledge applies it in some way. For example, an experienced gardener has years of gardening knowledge in his or her head, including how to plant various flowers and plants, when to plant them, how to cultivate and nurture them, how often to water them, and all of the knowledge related to gardening. The gardener also possesses the skills to translate that knowledge into action. The gardener knows when to plant seasonal flowers, how deep to plant, where to plant (in sunlight or in shade), how to water them, what insect spray to use, and all that it takes to grow and nurture annuals. If the gardener does not possess the knowledge for a particular kind of plant—roses, for example—she or he can refer to one of the recorded sources mentioned in item 1 above, or attend a class or consult another gardener who possesses that knowledge.

3. **The interaction and communication patterns among people** as they pursue their cultural, educational, informational, recreational, research, and economic activities. To transmit knowledge requires interaction between an information seeker and the information source, e.g., a person, book, journal article, class, or an Internet web site. The sources of the stored knowledge must be accessed in order to become part of an individual's knowledge base, and that transfer of knowledge requires interaction. We call this *information transfer or knowledge transfer*. The transfer of knowledge to an individual or group is the objective of the information professional.

4. **The values that have been adopted by a group of people.** What the group or sub-society consider important governs their acceptance of information and knowledge, as well as their laws and how they conduct themselves within society. Value systems can vary considerably among groups of people. For example, the values of a small community in the mountains of Colorado may differ considerably from the values of a metropolitan community in New York state. The values within a state or geographical region can vary based on the history of the community, its settlers, and the events that influenced the growth (or lack thereof) in the community over the years.

All four of these elements comprise the basic knowledge system in a community and greatly influence the new knowledge that is accepted in that community.

Social Knowledge and Information Services

In community analysis our objective is to identify the knowledge that people need in order to make their lives better and what information is needed to replace inaccurate knowledge and fill the gaps in a community's knowledge base. The information collections in libraries comprise potential knowledge that must be connected with the incomplete knowledge of clients. Each community and each individual possess a great deal of tacit knowledge, knowledge gained with experience and difficult to communicate. Tacit knowledge is stored in a human mind and usually cannot be captured as information to be transferred to others.

The model shown in Figure 3.1 is a very general portrayal of the individual and social knowledge that comprise a community knowledge infrastructure.

In this model, undiscovered knowledge consists of those questions, doubts, and gaps in knowledge that cause an individual to seek out information to fill the gaps or answer questions. Research is an attempt to identify those observations which would complement our understanding of phenomena and can be added to social knowledge as well as individual knowledge. In this sense, research creates knowledge by testing or discovering. That which is discovered is information that feeds into assumptions and hypotheses regarding the behavior and relationships of phenomena.

Because knowledge requires an understanding by a human mind, library collections attempt to complement individual knowledge with the information they contain. Community analysis attempts to identify the information needs or gaps in information for individuals, groups, and agencies, allowing

Figure 3.1   Knowledge in Society.

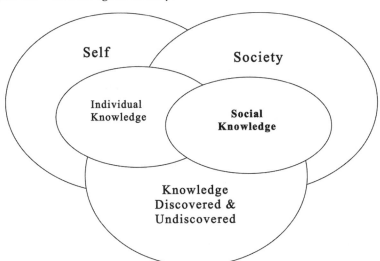

libraries to be more effective in meeting those needs and contributing to social knowledge.

Community analysis can also result in the production of additional social knowlege and information to fill gaps in the community information system. A library collects acceptable knowledge pertinent to a community's cultures. Community analysis is an attempt by library and information professionals to complement individual knowledge by making library collections and services available to address clientele needs and contribute to social knowledge. Therefore, a library's collection of recorded information becomes a vital part of a community's information infrastructure.

In summary, libraries and other information agencies connect individual knowledge with social knowledge, identifying information needs and extracting social knowledge to add to individual knowledge. By doing so, libraries are important elements of a community knowledge infrastructure.

Elements of a Community Knowledge Infrastructure

Societies create knowledge to reflect their universe, their culture, what they find acceptable, and what believable. We also tend to believe that there is more knowledge in people's heads than is documented. Communities without a tradition of writing are not well served by libraries. In the past, there has been an effort to educate peoples with oral cultures to fit into the mold of the societies that are currently served by libraries. These peoples must be assimilated into a print (recorded information) culture in order to use the resources.

Effective community analysis requires libraries to build networks to deal with social media; however, it is now possible to connect people through virtual communities of like-minded people sharing information that meets their common needs. All needs cannot be addressed only by the information held by libraries. In a community analysis we want to discover what knowledge people need to make their lives better—what information is needed to replace the inaccurate knowledge in their knowledge base. What we have collected in libraries is potential knowledge that must be connected with the incomplete knowledge of clientele. The information stored in libraries must be diffused to a person's mind in order for it to have meaning.

The professional activities associated with the knowledge infrastructure relate to the role of information and knowledge in society, from creation to ultimate preservation or discarding. As indicated earlier, information is defined as integrated data that is recorded. Information exists independently of any human intelligence and does not become knowledge until it is diffused into the mind of another person. Once information is incorporated in a human intelligence, it acquires meaning and can be used.

A model for conceptualizing the knowledge infrastructure is presented in Figure 3.2. The infrastructure is comprised of those individuals and agencies which participate in the creation, organization, diffusion, and use of knowledge.

The model in Figure 3.2 builds on extant knowledge that is continuously being created. Knowledge is an understanding of what will work, and using that understanding to solve a problem. Libraries and other information agencies help clientele use information to improve an activity or address a problem. Greer (Greer, Grover, and Fowler 2007) has articulated six functions of information and knowledge:

- Find or locate: The bibliographic (or identification) function of information
- Appreciate: The cultural function of information and books
- Teach or learn: The educational function of information and books
- Create new information or knowledge: The research function
- Decide: The informational function of information
- Enjoy: The recreational function

These functions of information and knowledge are explained in Chapter 12, in which we apply community analysis results to the design of information services.

Figure 3.2   The Knowledge Infrastructure.

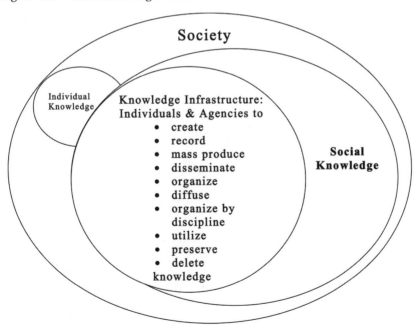

Libraries and other information agencies store and retrieve knowledge that people can process to complete gaps in their knowledge base. For example, a gardener may be able to use his or her personal body of knowledge in dealing with a certain plant or family of plants. If the gardener wishes to plant something different, he or she may go to a library to get sufficient information to expand his or her knowledge of general gardening to apply to this new plant which may require a different amount of sun, a certain amount of water, pruning, etc. In this scenario, the library takes the place of a neighbor who may have that knowledge. The gardener can go to the library to address a specialized need, adapting what is new to what he or she already knows.

FORMAL AND INFORMAL KNOWLEDGE SYSTEMS AND RESOURCES

Locating and retrieving information and knowledge can be accomplished by seeking both formal and informal sources of information. For example, talking to a neighbor is tapping into an informal system of information. Likewise, conversation at a gathering of friends or neighbors is informal information gathering. In such informal circumstances, the language used may also be informal and non-standardized, e.g., the specific names of plants, plant parts, fertilizers, and gardening techniques are familiar terms used in everyday language.

Enrolling in a class or workshop or going to a library are both examples of accessing established knowledge and require a knowledge of a specialized language and professional help to enter the knowledge system. The relationship is more logical and uses precise terms. An intermediary is necessary for the knowledge seeker to adapt to the formal knowledge system.

Librarians and information professionals, along with teachers and those trained in a knowledge system, assist novices as well as more expert knowledge seekers as they search for information. As technology becomes more sophisticated, it influences the knowledge infrastructure and facilitates access to less formal knowledge systems and resources. For example, Internet search engines such as Google bridge the gap between informal and formal systems by suggesting terms for use in a search.

The Relationship of Information Resources to Knowledge Systems

Books and databases do not reflect complete bodies of knowledge, which is what we carry in our minds, value-laden for decision making. Books and other packages of knowledge carry information that must be interpreted by humans in order to supplement our knowledge base. The gardener who understands the body of gardening knowledge can use that knowledge when planting a new crop; her or his understanding of gardening knowledge is relevant for the task. However, the gardener needs specialized information to augment existing knowledge when she or he ventures into a new aspect of gardening. The gardener in this example is learning by extracting information and knowledge from a knowledge resource to complete a new dimension of his or her understanding of horticulture.

Use as the Interface of Formal and Informal Knowledge Systems

The knowledge transfer process is influenced by variables external to that process. We call these variables "the environmental and social context." These variables apply to communities of all types and are listed below.

1. **Culture:** language, philosophical and moral values, the educational system, concept of time, historical background, and all features which comprise a community's culture.
2. **Physical geography:** aspects such as climate and topographical characteristics.
3. **Political structure of society:** the system for governance and underlying values regarding the role of government in a dynamic society.
4. **Legislation:** policy and regulations issued by the legislative and regulatory agencies of government.
5. **The economic system:** under which the culture functions.
6. **Technology:** the level of sophistication in terms of computer and telecommunication technology.
7. **Information policy:** copyright laws, policies regarding secrecy, censorship, privacy, ownership, the public's right to know, and the government's responsibility to inform.

These variables in the community's environment influence all aspects of the knowledge transfer process. These environmental variables and the explanation below are adapted from the authors' earlier work (Greer, Grover, and Fowler 2007, 53–57).

Culture

While we often think of culture very broadly, as in the culture of an ethnic group or country, we can also think of culture as it applies to communities or organizations, as we suggested above. The local idioms, food, entertainment, history, and dress of rural Kansas vary considerably from the culture of New Orleans or New York City. The corporate culture of IBM varies considerably from that of WalMart. In different cultures, attitudes vary, along with the meanings associated with language and information.

These factors influence how people perceive information and knowledge—how they think.

Physical Geography

The geography and climate of a community influence the community's lifestyle, use of leisure time, and culture. California and the American south both boast a climate that encourages outdoor activities most of the year, including the winter months. While residents of southern California, the Southwest, the Gulf Coast, and Florida are playing tennis on weekends, those in the rest of the country are indoors watching movies on DVD, bowling, attending basketball games, or otherwise staying indoors during the winter. The weather influences recreational activities, and differences in lifestyle influence attitudes as well as needs for information and knowledge.

Political Structure

The system of governance in a community or organization influences the flow of information. A hierarchy generally requires that information flow up and down the organization according to the rank of the individual. An organization that is more informal usually encourages information flow in a more casual manner, without regard to the status of the sender or the receiver. In such organizations, information flow can be fast, and unencumbered by status.

Political structure can also influence the content of information. For example, the values of a dominant political party may suppress information that is opposed to the prevailing views, and this suppressed information may find an outlet through "underground" or illicit channels. This political structure may be dictated by the culture of the organization and by the leadership style of those in leadership positions. Similarly, the format of the information may be dictated by the political structure, e.g., print being preferred to electronic sources; narrative being preferred to charts or diagrams.

Some leaders subscribe to an organizational philosophy that information must be controlled and that power or authority is derived from the control of information. Other leaders may believe that information should be shared among leaders and among all workers. These sharing leaders will treat new information in a manner much different than those who wish to control. In these examples, the philosophy of management focuses on the locus of control, and that control is determined to a large extent by access to information. How information and knowledge are controlled and distributed is largely dependent on leadership style and philosophy.

Legislation and Regulations

Legislation and regulations are issued by the legislative and regulatory agencies of government. Where the political paradigm is controlled by the scope and limits of a constitution, such as by the U.S. Constitution, freedom of access to information is at the core of this paradigm and is the bedrock of any information system designed for public use. The U.S. Constitution guarantees in the First Amendment the right of free expression of ideas, and other laws, e.g., copyright law, also protect individuals or groups who create new packages of information so that others cannot steal those ideas and call them their own.

Copyright protects various forms of expression, including songs and music, as well as prose and poetry. Similarly, patents protect the rights of inventors who create new products of various kinds, including hardware and software which may access, organize, store, or retrieve information. Still other laws, such as securities laws, provide a framework for the exchange of stock information, determining when this information can be exchanged fairly, and when it is considered illegal "insider" trading of information.

Economic System

The economic system supports a culture and social system financially. If capitalism is the basis for economic activity in a society, information is seen as a commodity that appears in the marketplace as well as in the halls of the academies. Privacy and proprietary perspectives are very evident in this society. Other economic systems, e.g., communism, employ different approaches to the creation, reproduction, and distribution of information.

In a capitalistic society, the marketplace determines the marketability of a product. Because information and knowledge are commodities, the format and content of information and knowledge are influenced substantially by the economic feasibility of the information package. For example, the marketability of a new information system, such as the Internet, must be accompanied by affordable accessibility. The Internet was created in the 1960s by the U.S. government to exchange defense information, using state-of-the-art computers, software, and networking technologies. This system was not available to the public until personal computers, telecommunications, and software became affordable to regional, state, and local government agencies and private individuals. The widespread availability of the Internet became a reality in the mid-1990s with the confluence of technology and affordability.

Often the diffusion process occurs first through the diffusion of information for recreation, followed by use for educational purposes. The use of film, audio recordings, compact discs, and digital video all found their way into the marketplace first as entertainment packages. To anticipate changes in technology applications, information professionals are advised to watch trends in the use of new technologies for entertainment as possible precursors of technology use for other purposes.

Technology

The level of sophistication for computer and telecommunication technology becomes increasingly relevant to the processes of information and knowledge transfer in a society. As noted above, the application of new technology to the transfer of information is dictated by economics. Affordability precedes adaptation on a wide scale in society.

Technological innovation has transformed all aspects of information creation, recording, mass production, distribution, organization, storage, retrieval, and use. With the rapid changes in technology, transfer of information has been changed dramatically. The ability to transmit information using cell phone technologies, to store and retrieve information on palmtop computers, and the availability of instant messaging has had a major impact on daily life and on the practice of the information professions.

Information Policy

Copyright laws, policies regarding secrecy, censorship, privacy, ownership, the public's right to know, and the government's responsibility to inform are examples of information policy. Legislation is a formal policy adopted by a governmental body at the local, state, national, or international level and is addressed in the "legislation and regulation" section of our discussion. Those laws and regulations which specifically address the creation, production, distribution, use, and storage of information may also be considered information policy. However, policy may be adopted within small and large agencies and groups of all types.

A policy is a generalization or general statement which provides guidelines for the transfer or use of information. For example, any social organization, school, library, college or university, business, or government agency at any level may articulate a policy of information use. A small business may elect to keep no papers or financial records after seven years, because tax records must be kept for seven years. Another small business, conscious of its historic contribution to a community, may elect to preserve all correspondence and donate them after five years to a local historical museum. While the practices outlined are much different, they are both policies which govern the transfer of information for their respective agencies and are consistent with their culture.

All of the above variables influence each other and, in turn, influence the information professional's role in the transfer of information and knowledge.

IMPLICATIONS FOR ASSESSING INFORMATION
NEEDS AND CUSTOMIZING INFORMATION SERVICES

The professional activities associated with the knowledge infrastructure relate to the role of information and knowledge in society, from creation to ultimate preservation or discarding. As indicated earlier, information is defined as integrated data that has been recorded. That is, it exists independently of any human intelligence and does not convert to knowledge until it is diffused into the intellect of another person. Once information is incorporated in to a human intelligence, it acquires meaning and can be used.

The sum total of what a community knows constitutes the resources that libraries tap into to enhance individuals' abilities to address their problems. Through information needs analysis, information professionals identify subject areas where people have inadequate knowledge to fulfill their roles or enact their projects. Through role theory we can predict the information needs of individuals or groups according to their roles in their communities. If we understand the mission of organizations and agencies, we can know what knowledge these organizations are using, and through questions directed toward information seekers in the organization, we can identify gaps and meet their needs. Likewise, we can identify the gaps in an individual's information or knowledge needs and compare those gaps with the community knowledge available through the library. We can then compare the individual's known information needs to library records, and provide the community knowledge to close the gap.

The role of library and information professionals in creating a knowledge infrastructure is portrayed in Figure 3.3. The vertical axis, representing the information infrastructure, is the traditional role of libraries—aiding to a greater or lesser extent in the creation, recording, mass production, dissemination, organization, diffusion, utilization, preservation, and deletion of information in its variety of formats. By systematically assessing the customers' needs, library and information professionals can more effectively promote the diffusion of information, assisting in the diffusion of knowledge and the enhancement of a community's knowledge infrastructure.

The model in Figure 3.3 can be used to calculate the position of a library in relation to the customization of information services and its contributions to the knowledge infrastructure. The nine points on the vertical scale represent aspects of the information transfer cycle, and each point can be used to estimate on a scale of 1 (low) to 5 (high) the degree of customization at that point, e.g., if the library regularly assesses clientele needs in designing services that enable people to use information effectively, that library might score 4 or 5 in the utilization category. By looking at the scores for each category, library staff can gain a clearer understanding of the library's current practices for customizing its information services. A high score suggests a

Figure 3.3   A Model for Assessing Information Services.

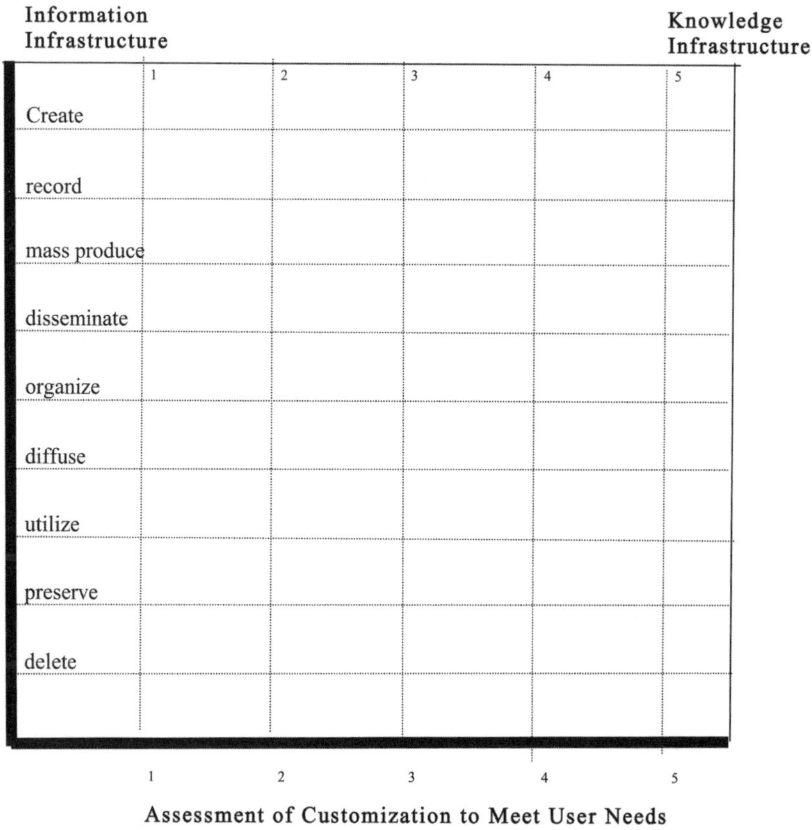

Information   **Knowledge**
Infrastructure   **Infrastructure**

	1	2	3	4	5
Create					
record					
mass produce					
disseminate					
organize					
diffuse					
utilize					
preserve					
delete					

            1   2   3   4   5

Assessment of Customization to Meet User Needs

library that is a vital part of the knowledge infrastructure, a transformative library.

Librarians and other information professionals work to complement people's knowledge in order to fulfill their needs. They can also teach clientele the skills to independently retrieve information; we call these skills *information literacy*. It is at this point where information counseling comes in and diagnosis occurs. A library that successfully and continuously provides information literacy services is a transformative library.

After an information needs assessment we can identify the lack of availability of adequate resources. The professionals who identify that gap are obliged to locate needed resources or support research to fill the gap. If there is knowledge in the community but there is an ineffective information or knowledge infrastructure, the librarian must create ways to transfer information and knowledge to those who need it.

An example of inadequate information infrastructure exists in indigenous cultures. Indigenous people may not have the technology to fulfill the functions of an information infrastructure. Information professionals would have the responsibility to develop the components of that infrastructure, employing appropriate technologies and processes to address the unique needs of the culture.

SUMMARY

Library and information professionals have an integral role to play in a community's knowledge system, which includes the individuals and agencies comprising the knowledge infrastructure. Effective information agencies identify gaps in the knowledge of individuals, groups, and organizations and provide the knowledge that fills those gaps. In order to diagnose information needs, information professionals must get to know their communities through a continuous, systematic community analysis process, a necessary component for transformative libraries.

REFERENCES

Cleveland, Harlan. 1985. *The knowledge executive; leadership in an information society.* New York: Truman Talley Books/E. P. Dutton.

Glazier, Jack D. and Robert Grover. 2002. A Multidisciplinary Framework for Theory Building. In *Current theory in library and information science*, Issue ed.William E. McGrath. *Library Trends 50* no. 3, 317–329.

Greer, Roger C., Robert J. Grover, and Susan G. Fowler. 2007. *Introduction to the library and information professions.* Westport, CT: Libraries Unlimited.

Mason, Robert. 2007. "Culture: An Overlooked Key to Unlocking Organizational Knowledge." In *Cross-cultural perspectives on knowledge management*, ed. David J. Pauleen, 21–34. Westport, CT and London: Libraries Unlimited.

Wilson, Patrick. 1977. *Public knowledge, private ignorance; toward a library and information policy.* Westport, CT and London: Greenwood Press.

CHAPTER 4

The Theoretical Framework for Community Analysis

CHAPTER OVERVIEW

This chapter describes the Community Analysis Research Institute (CARI) model and its values. The tension between change and preservation of the status quo is discussed, along with the need for reconceptualizing values in order to provide successful customer-centered information services. The role of the information professional is to diagnose information needs, and community analysis is essential to that process. The social science theories that support community analysis are described briefly to provide information professionals with a basis for making decisions that affect clientele.

THE ROLE OF THE INFORMATION PROFESSIONAL

A professional of any kind possesses specialized knowledge that enables the application of that knowledge on behalf of a client. The role of any professional, e.g., physician, librarian, teacher, or financial planner, is that of diagnosing needs, prescribing a service to meet those needs, implementing that service, and evaluating the outcome of this interaction (Greer, Grover, and Fowler 2007).

The Service Cycle

In most professions, this process is accomplished at two levels, with individuals and with groups, as indicated in Figure 4.1.

Figure 4.1   The Diagnostic Process.

For Individuals	For Groups
Diagnosis	Analysis
Prescription	Recommendation
Treatment	Implementation
Evaluation	Evaluation

This process, which we call the "service cycle," will be described below as it applies to an information professional, and is based on the medical model for diagnosis. The reader is urged not to dwell on the different terms used to distinguish the diagnostic processes for individuals and groups. The different terminology is used merely to emphasize the distinction between individual and group services.

Diagnosis

The information professional must be able to assess the information needs of a clientele at two levels: (1) analyzing the characteristics of the community or area served; and (2) analyzing the needs of specific individuals at the point when and where they seek information from the library. The diagnostic process is explored in more detail below.

Prescription

The professional practitioner, in a one-on-one relationship with a client, will recommend or "prescribe" appropriate sources in which the desired information may be located, analyzed, and integrated to satisfy the diagnosed need. On the other hand, the professional as a manager approaches the diagnosis/prescription process from an organizational perspective. That is, the process is not intended to serve the needs of a single person only, but rather, the entire population within the library service area. The needs assessment is an analysis of aggregated data about the population of the service area and is used to create an organization customized in its design, collections, and services to fit the characteristics, behaviors, and idiosyncrasies of that population. Conclusions from this analysis can lead to informed decisions about such specifics as the size and scope of children's collections and services, or the number and types of video and audio cassettes in the collection.

Treatment or Implementation

The treatment or implementation stage is the retrieval, organization, and integration of the information or service that has been prescribed, suggested, or recommended. At the one-on-one level of service, the treatment brings the client and the needed information together. This service requires knowledge of various information sources and services that are available within the systems, as well as those located elsewhere. With the advancement of more complex and sophisticated technology, the library and information professional must be aware of (1) the array of information sources available, (2) the best use of a particular information package for meeting client needs, (3) the preferred formats of the client, and (4) the information needs of the client.

Evaluation

After the treatment or recommendation has been implemented, the outcome must be evaluated in terms of the client's resolution and satisfaction. An imperfect or unsatisfactory resolution of the original need or requirement must trigger a repetition of the entire cycle. The second cycle may only amend a small part of the whole sequence, or may require an entirely new approach. In a reference situation, for example, the librarian would observe and query the client after presenting a piece of information to assess the appropriateness of the information provided. Likewise, a type of service, for example a local information and referral database, should be evaluated and modified according to the findings of a valuative process. Similarly, allocations of organization resources for specific purposes need to be evaluated at predetermined points after implementation. Methods for collecting and analyzing data for purposes of evaluation can range from simple verbal inquiries to sophisticated quantitative statistical analyses, depending upon the circumstances.

The Diagnostic Process in Information Services

The diagnosis of an individual's information need typically occurs through a communication process with the individual information user. Usually called the reference interview, this is a communication process during which the information user's needs can be identified and one or more sources of needed information can be recommended.

This process is not linear, although the previous discussion and Figure 4.1 might suggest that it is. Instead, it is an iterative process, as shown in Figure 4.2. After the evaluation of an interview or service, the cycle begins again, using knowledge gained from the previous diagnosis, prescription, treatment, and evaluation. The process is more accurately portrayed as a circle.

As shown in the figure, the diagnostic process occurs at two levels: (1) analyzing the characteristics of the community or area served; and (2) analyzing the needs of specific individuals.

Figure 4.2   The Diagnostic Cycle.

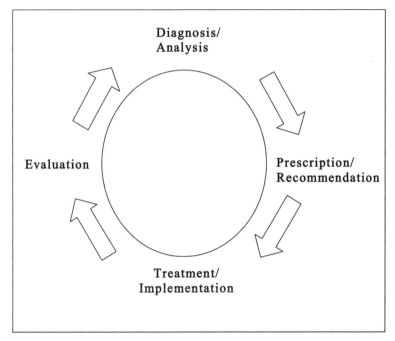

The purpose of the first level of analysis, community analysis, is to provide the professional (as a manager) with specific data about the community and its residents. Knowledge acquired through a systematic process of data collection and analysis enables the library manager to understand the context or environment in which the library operates. This understanding will provide a conceptual framework for the customization of collections, services, and space allocations. The primary methodology for data collection and analysis is a systematic process enhanced by intuition, impressions, observations, interviews and common sense. This level of diagnosis is a first critical step in customizing library and information service for individuals and groups.

The second level of diagnosis is a one-on-one interaction with a user at the point when and where the decision has been made to seek information to resolve an uncertainty. At the *technician* level of service, the user is expected to have made his or her own diagnosis, and the technician retrieves the relevant material or directs the user to the appropriate source. The technician is expected to have a knowledge of the information system and the resources within the system.

At the **professional** level of service, understanding the exact information needs of the user is the first step in the professional/client interaction. At this point, the professional initiates a diagnostic process with the client as well as accepting responsibility for the outcome. This interrogation must begin with the basic questions of what, why, how much, when, etc., and be narrowed to fit the professional's perceptions of the client's level of literacy, cognitive style, social and cultural construction of reality, and other personal attributes which will influence information use. Once this level of assessment of need is derived, the **professional** will proceed to the next stage of the service cycle, i.e., prescribing, suggesting, or recommending the source or sources from which the appropriate information may be acquired.

The interview must take into account the individual differences of the client, such as cognitive style and preferences for format. Unfortunately, the reference interview often is not viewed from the perspective of the user. As noted by Kuhlthau (2004), information systems typically have been guided by the bibliographic paradigm that views information use from the information system's perspective. An "information system" refers to a library, information center, or other information agency.

THE DEFINITION OF "COMMUNITY ANALYSIS"

Customizing information services to address information needs requires a knowledge of the clientele, in this case communities. To customize services to communities we must systematically collect data about the community in order to infer the information needs; however, a community is a very complex organization. How do we grapple with this complexity? The community analysis model divides data collection into four parts. First let's define community analysis.

We will use the definition developed by Greer and Hale (1982, 358) as they analyzed the information needs of more than two dozen communities and participated in the process in over 300 communities around the United States:

> Community analysis is a systematic process of collecting, organizing and analyzing data about the library and its environment. It is designed to assist the administrator in choosing from among alternative patterns of satisfying residents' information needs and interests.

This process of assessing a community's needs applies to any definition of a community: a municipality, a university, a corporation, a government agency, or a school system. Likewise, the model for community analysis outlined here can also apply to any definition of community.

Evolution of the Greer Community Analysis Model

The community analysis model described in this book was first developed by Roger Greer in the early 1970s through a contract with the New York State Development Corporation. Greer agreed to analyze the community of Baldwinsville, New York and determine whether a planned new community should develop its library services as part of the Baldwinsville system or be developed independently.

Greer, while pursuing his doctorate, was influenced by Rutgers professors Ralph Shaw, Lowell Martin, Mary Gaver, and Paul Duncan. Greer was also influenced by Georg Schneider's (1961) book on the history and theory of bibliography, and the writings of Jesse Shera. Shera focused on information users to develop programs of service for communities. When assigned to teach bibliography, Greer thought about the differences between systematic bibliography, which seeks to compile an inventory of works within a given scope, descriptive bibliography, which centers on the book as physical object, and subject bibliography, which focuses on user needs and development of a bibliography to meet those needs.

While teaching bibliographic control to master's degree students, his assigned term paper required students to create a bibliography that met defined client needs. Students were required to write an introduction which explained who the audience was, what that audience's needs were, and how the student would organize the bibliography to meet the needs of this audience. It was specified as a subject bibliography, customized to be totally user-centered. While teaching the course in bibliographic control of information, Greer developed his conceptual framework through bibliography.

For the contract for the Baldwinsville community, Greer worked with Dan O'Connor, a doctoral student at Syracuse University at that time. Greer searched the professional literature for a model to follow for studying community information needs, but none was found in the library literature or the literature associated with public relations, marketing, or sociology.

Early in his thinking about analyzing a community, Greer knew that he could use census data for baseline community data. He concluded that the typical public library user was an individual. A study of the population of the Baldwinsville community showed that the community was a highly organized assembly of individuals who coalesced into a variety of groups to share and achieve common interests or goals. He noted further that, unlike identifying the information needs of individuals, identifying the information needs of groups was relatively easy. Furthermore, data about groups provided more evidence about the needs and interests of the individuals in the community.

A third variable that provided insight into the characteristics of the population of a community was the "agencies" that were created and that existed to serve the needs of the individuals. These agencies included corporate entities and retail businesses, along with medical, educational, governmental, and religious agencies. Knowing the composite makeup of these agencies and the purposes they served in the community provided another source of information about the individuals.

A fourth perspective was the systematic examination of a community's culture. This area was felt to be another vital part of a community's individuality, and the term "lifestyles" was used to designate this fourth variable in community information needs analysis. This included information that was not easily quantifiable, such as political orientation or recreational activities.

Thus, Greer's model identified four variables, or perspectives, of a community which may be studied to obtain a comprehensive understanding of a community and its population: individuals, groups, agencies, and lifestyles. This model for community analysis variables is shown in Figure 4.3.

Figure 4.3   Community Analysis Model.

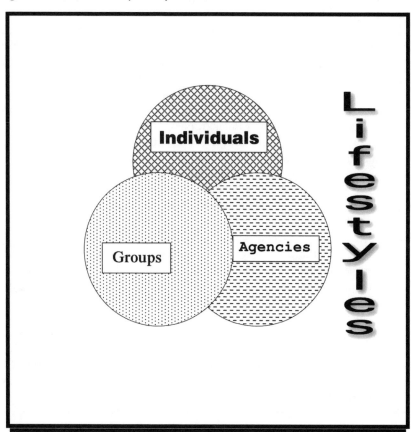

The primary sources of information for these four categories are: (1) census data for individuals; (2) local newspapers for information on groups and lifestyles; and (3) an area phone book for information about corporate groups and other agencies. Data collected were drawn from these existing sources rather than from surveys, interviews, or other forms of data collection. Greer believed that the four perspectives would provide a comprehensive picture of the community. If further confirmation of conclusions was required, generating data through customized surveys and other research efforts could be developed.

Based upon results of the Baldwinsville study, and because there was no practical model yet available, Greer developed a workshop to teach librarians how to conduct a community analysis using these four perspectives. This workshop model was used for a three-day conference funded by the U.S. Department of Education at Syracuse University. Staffs from 17 library systems in the Northeast and Mid-Atlantic states were selected to attend the workshop. Each library system sent a trustee or community official, a senior staff manager, and a third member (staff or volunteer) who would lead a group to conduct the process.

Following the success of the workshop, Greer concluded that he could develop a seminar for advanced master's students and teach the community analysis methodology during an academic semester. He recruited students at Syracuse University School of Information Studies to replicate the Baldwinsville study in the Onondaga Hill Public Library in one semester. Following that study, he did another community analysis at a branch of the Syracuse Public Library, and a fourth at Pulaski, New York.

It was during this time that Greer realized that the circulation file had enormous value as a source to discern information on what library resources the clientele are using. The registration file traditionally was a tool used to recover items borrowed and overdue. Greer concluded that the registration process was the single most important encounter between the client and the library and it should therefore be exploited, within the boundaries of privacy, to identify the general and particular information needs of the borrower.

The success of the three-day conference encouraged Greer to sign contracts with state libraries to give more three-day workshops. It became evident that the "how to" could be taught in an afternoon, but the "why" (the philosophy supporting library services) took much longer.

The community analysis model relied on newspapers to identify change in a community as one part of the process. Converting to a user orientation required "standing outside the library" to gain an understanding of the community and the place of the library in that community. This perspective differed from the concept of service in the early 1970s. Service was still an administrative function; librarians provided a service because they had the staff and resources to do those things that libraries could do. Service was based more on the nature of the resources available than on known user needs.

The early community analyses defined the following guiding principles:

1. Community change, including changing library services, requires understanding of the past and present.
2. Theories from psychology, sociology, and education are applied as necessary for effective analysis of a community.
3. The person who lives in the community can use intuition to bring understanding to community analysis, enabling anticipation of needs. Librarians and staff can bring meaning to information collected because they intuitively understand the history and culture of the community, which influence information needs.
4. The four perspectives of a community can be applied to any type of community.

Component Parts of the CARI Model

As noted above, this community analysis model identifies four categories for analysis, and each is described briefly here. A chapter is devoted to each category later in the book.

Individuals

This aspect of community analysis examines a community through its demographics. A look at census data reveals an analysis of such variables as the population of the municipality and the ethnic makeup of the community, or the socioeconomic makeup. Characteristics that are informative in the analysis of individuals within a population, and that can be attained from recent census data for municipalities, include such data as age, family structure, education level, employment, and other economic characteristics.

The examples above for municipalities can be easily adapted to other kinds of communities as well. The communities of colleges, schools, private enterprises, and government agencies can be analyzed in the same way, as explained in more detail in Chapter 6.

Groups

A second variable in the CARI model for analyzing communities is **groups**. The information professional conducting an information needs assessment may identify various groups in the community and their information needs.

The definition of groups for our purposes is "a formal or informal organization which meets and functions regularly." Unlike an agency, a group does not necessarily have an office or telephone for contact. Examples of groups in a community would be service organizations (Lions Clubs,

Rotary, etc.), service fraternities and sororities, and clubs such as informal bird watchers' clubs. In smaller communities, the local newspaper often includes news of local clubs and meeting schedules, and many groups have a web site and/or accounts on such social media as Facebook and Twitter.

In a school community, the groups would include school student organizations, e.g., marching band, debate club, science club, photography club, and other organizations that cater to student interests. Other groups might be faculty-teaching teams, the parent-teachers association, school board, and, in larger systems, principals and department chairs may meet as groups.

Agencies

While groups are usually informal organizations, **agencies** are formal parts of a larger organization, and these agencies generally provide services or products to residents of the community. For example, a community will have such agencies as police and fire departments, a public library, human resources department, recreation department, schools, health services, churches, and numerous other agencies that have a mission within the municipality. A community analysis requires assessing information needs by identifying and analyzing the missions and characteristics of agencies serving the community. Agencies are discussed in depth in Chapter 8.

Lifestyles

The fourth category of our community analysis model is lifestyles. This term refers to the unique culture of a community: its history, values, customs, traditions, topography, climate, leisure activities, and other attributes that make the community unique.

The components of lifestyle can influence the types of information services offered in a community of any type: municipality, academic environment, school library, or special library clientele. This vital part of the community analysis model is discussed in Chapter 9.

The four perspectives of a community analysis outlined above will enable the information professional to identify the unique qualities of a community and to identify agencies and groups who are leading contributors to the lifestyle of the community. It is a systematic approach for collecting data for making decisions abut information services to be offered. The process for collecting data is discussed in Chapter 10, "Implementing a Community Analysis."

ADAPTING TO COMMUNITY CHANGE

Change is a constant in any community, whether a city, company, college, or school system. People move in and move out. Roles in the community and community leadership change. A change of leaders, especially high-level leadership, can result in a change in philosophy, strategies, values, policies, and leadership and management style. The national and local economies influence prices; therefore, budgets must be adjusted. New laws at the national, state, and local levels require changes in management, budgeting, and policies. Severe weather can severely impact budgets, schedules, and productivity. All of these changes, and others, have an impact on the information organization itself, as well as on the clientele.

Because no organization or community is static, information professionals must be alert to change—change in political structure of the community, economics, legislation, policies—especially information policy, and environmental factors, including weather, transportation, living conditions. To monitor these changes, information professionals must be intelligent consumers of the news by reading and viewing daily local, regional, state, and national news sources—newspapers, news magazines, and commentaries which are readily online and broadcast on radio or television. Since news organizations have become more sensational and biased in recent years, it is more important than ever to systematically scan several sources of news to stay current and aware of all aspects of controversial issues.

Local issues are especially important to monitor, as they can have the most immediate impact on the community. Local issues can also be the most challenging to identify and confront if that community does not have a news reporting organization. For suburbs, schools, smaller colleges, and small communities of all types, the information professional must tune in to both formal and informal sources of information. Formal sources include the public affairs office and the administration of an organization and official publications, web sites, and blogs. Informal sources include "the grapevine": informal networks, lunchroom conversations, and hallway encounters. All of these sources are necessary to stay current with local community dynamics.

Once aware of the changing facets of a community, the information professional must continuously assess the impact of change on a community's information needs. What services are needed to address new issues? Knowledge of the community's history is helpful in addressing this question.

Community Change Requires Understanding the Past and Present

Monitoring current changes is important, but understanding the impact on the community requires knowledge of the community's "big picture," its historical context. All of the methods for gathering information described in this book will provide information useful for decision-making. However, the decision-making is most effective when the current situation, including recent changes, is understood in the context of the community's history. That history is a part of lifestyle, which is discussed in a later chapter.

Information professionals can learn a lot about a community's history by talking with long-time residents. These conversations help to build a network for continuous assessment of change, awareness of current issues, and a history of how the community got to its present state.

Social Science Theories Are Necessary for Effective Analysis of a Community

Theory provides the foundation for professional practice. We believe that it cannot be emphasized enough that the object of professional service is to create and deliver customized products to a specified clientele, whether an individual, group, community, organization, or society. Customization is a process wherein each product is fashioned to satisfy the identified or diagnosed needs of a client. To distinguish the customized product of a professional from the efforts of a talented and well-meaning layperson or technician requires the application of theory.

Theory has been described as "generalizations that seek to explain relationships among phenomena." (Glazier and Grover 2002, 319) Theory helps us understand why things happen and helps us to anticipate what will happen when similar circumstances are present at a different time. For example, Newton's theory of gravity says that any object which leaves the surface of the earth is drawn back down. (A more detailed discussion of professional level theory is found in Greer, Grover, and Fowler 2007.)

Professional theory represents the body of knowledge a profession acquires over time. This acquisition may be by a variety of means, from vigorous scientific study to accumulated layers of anecdotal experiences. Its function is to provide guidance in deriving meaning from information acquired during the diagnostic process. Once the meaning associated with data is understood, theory may also provide direction and parameters for the development of the service to satisfy the needs of the client.

Another objective of theory is to predict an outcome when certain characteristics are present. In the case of human behavior, the goal of prediction is less attainable than in the areas of the physical and biological sciences. Nevertheless, identification of trends is a meaningful function of theory and serves in the diagnostic process.

The library and other information professions are far-reaching in the range of service provided. In some positions, information professionals have wide-ranging responsibilities, e.g., school library media specialists, public librarians in smaller libraries, and one-person libraries. Other information professionals are specialized, e.g., map librarians, archivists, law librarians, corporate librarians, acquisition librarians, reference librarians, research specialists, catalogers, and music librarians. Because of their responsibilities, information professionals may be called librarians, information specialists, researchers, archivists, information brokers, information entrepreneurs, or other such terms.

All of these information professionals share the following characteristics, which were first described by Greer (1987, 7) and were adapted and updated by Greer, Grover, and Fowler (2007). The characteristics are briefly summarized here.

1. Responsibility for the commodity "information" and the objective of enhancing the processes of information transfer.
2. Responsibility for accommodating the information needs and behavioral characteristics of a specific client population.
3. Responsibility for the design and management of an organization consisting of staff, equipment, space and financial resources to provide the interface between the information system and the potential user.
4. Responsibility for the design and management of an information system encompassing a database, a collection of information in any format.

The knowledge required to carry out these shared characteristics is the knowledge base for the library and information professions, the science of the information professions. This theory base is amplified in the discussion that follows.

THE SCIENCE OF THE INFORMATION PROFESSIONS

The science of the information professions may be properly called "information science." However, that term, "information science," is also frequently used to designate the application of technology to the acquisition, storage, retrieval, and dissemination of information.

While some aspects of this science are consistent with the so-called hard sciences, for the most part its domain is related to the social sciences, specifically the psychological and sociological perspectives. Consequently, information science quite rightly belongs within the family of disciplines commonly associated with the social sciences.

Information science seeks to address the four common areas of focus of information professionals outlined above by posing the following questions (we identify the related field of study in parentheses):

1. How is knowledge converted to information, reproduced, and disseminated to society (the sociology information)?
2. How do individuals seek and acquire information (information psychology)?
3. How are organizations for the management of information organized and managed (management of information organizations)?
4. How are databases developed and maintained for a particular purpose (information engineering)?

Our objective here is to explore the fields of Information Psychology and Sociology of Information that belong within the discipline of information science, following the model first articulated by Greer (1987). Each exploration will include a description of the scope of the field.

Information Psychology

The goal of information professionals is to create and operate information systems and services to accommodate the information needs and behavioral characteristics of a specific client population. This goal of customizing information service requires knowledge of human behavior associated with the acquisition and use of information. Information psychology is the field of information science concerned with the development of this theory of human behavior. Information psychology applies behavioral theory to the library and information professions in the same way that educational psychology applies psychology theory to the education professions.

Knowledge of an individual's way of processing of information is vital to the identification of information sources to meet the needs of that individual. Likewise, knowledge of information psychology is required for a library and information professional to design and implement an information service that addresses the information needs and preferences of individuals.

The field of information psychology addresses the following questions:

1. How does a person decide that he or she has a need for information? What are the conditions or motives that provoke this awareness?
2. What processes are involved in decisions to satisfy or ignore the need?
3. What strategies are employed in searching for information, and how do these strategies differ among individuals?
4. What are the variations in behaviors associated with the search for information? How does the configuration of the use of a particular information system affect these behaviors?
5. How does the medium of the information (book, electronic publication, video, etc.) influence the individual's selection and use of the information?
6. What methods and criteria are employed in evaluating the relevance of the information acquired?
7. What are the behaviors associated with the processes of assimilating information? How does information become knowledge? How do format and system design affect this aspect of behavior?
8. What cognitive styles are employed in information processing? How does an individual's learning style influence information searching, information retrieval, and information use?
9. How do individuals organize, store, and retrieve information from memory?

10. What are the varieties of forms and patterns of information utilization?

Contributing to an understanding of these questions are the research and theory from the following fields:

1. Behavioral psychology, including personality theory, perception theory, motivation theory, attitude theory, cognitive science, theories of intelligence, role theory, learning theory
2. Psycho-linguistics
3. Physiology
4. Religion
5. Educational psychology
6. Social psychology
7. Sociology of information
8. Information engineering
9. Information organization management

As noted above, role theory contributes to an understanding of the information user's needs. Role theory is a sub-discipline of psychology that studies the activity of people as they spend much of their time in groups. In the groups, these individuals engage in expected behaviors and take certain positions. Each of these positions is called a role. Each role that an individual fulfills suggests their possible information needs. For example, the role of parent suggests a need for information about children: their health, diet, psychology, recreation, education, and other aspects of child rearing. Similarly, an occupational or professional role implies other needs that drive the individual's need for information, such as continuing education for a career.

Both information psychology and the sociology of information provide the background knowledge that enables a library and information professional to conduct an effective information needs assessment. Information psychology provides the knowledge of how individuals use information; the sociology of information provides insight from the perspective of an individual's membership in a group.

The Sociology of Information

The study of the role of information in society and the systems, processes, and patterns of information transfer draw its perspectives from the discipline of sociology. This field, which we call the sociology of information, must address issues associated with the creation of knowledge, its recording and reproduction, and the various social systems involved in its dissemination and utilization. This field seeks to understand and predict the steps involved in the creation, recording, mass production, dissemination, collection, organization, storage, retrieval, preservation, discarding and destruction of information in society.

The activities associated with the sociology of information relate to the role of information in society, from creation to ultimate preservation or discarding. As indicated earlier, information is defined as knowledge recorded, i.e., it exists independently of any human intelligence and does not become knowledge until it is diffused into the intellect of another person. Once information is incorporated in a human intelligence, it acquires meaning and may become a building block toward wisdom.

The social processes of this field are reflected in the following questions:

1. What are the patterns of knowledge creation? How is new knowledge created? What are the accepted research methods?
2. What are the systems for recording knowledge? As research is conducted and new knowledge is created, how are the data recorded? What technologies are used in the recording process?
3. What are the mechanisms for the mass production of information? After research is completed, how is this research packaged for distribution to a large audience? What are the accepted presses for publishing? Which electronic media are used?
4. Which varieties of systems are employed in the dissemination of information? When the new knowledge has been packaged for mass distribution, what are the professional associations, professional conferences, publishers, conferences, mass media, and web sites used to distribute the new knowledge?
5. What systems for bibliographic control of the records are being produced in society? What are the bibliographies, webographies, indexes, and other organizing tools that organize knowledge in this area and make it available to audiences?
6. What is the paradigmatic structure for the organization of information by subject fields? Within each specialty area, how does this knowledge fit into the discipline or profession? What special terms are used to organize and retrieve this knowledge?
7. What are the patterns of diffusion of knowledge? How and through what social organizations is this new knowledge likely to be taught to others? What are the leading universities or other social agencies that specialize in passing on new knowledge in the field?
8. How is information used in society? What are the likely user groups who would put this new knowledge to use?
9. What systems exist for the preservation of information? Which agencies are likely to preserve this knowledge? What means would be used to maintain the knowledge?

Among the fields of study which contribute to an understanding of sociology of information are the following:

1. Sociology, including sociology of knowledge and symbolic interactionism
2. Economics
3. Intellectual history
4. Political science
5. Cultural anthropology
6. Cybernetics
7. Bibliometrics
8. Socio-linguistics
9. Information psychology
10. Information engineering
11. Information organization management

These theories, or areas of knowledge, help the information professional to understand how individuals and groups use information. This knowledge is critical for designing information services.

SUMMARY

The complexity of social research required for new understandings in library and information science implies study in a diverse body of knowledge to understand the human condition. Because the focus of research by information professionals must include human behavior in its myriad manifestations relating to information and information transfer, research models must draw upon the disciplines within the family of social and behavioral science for methodologies that can generate applicable theory. Human behavior can be better understood through the study of such social science disciplines as history, anthropology, psychology, sociology, communication, ethnography, and linguistics. The study of information systems can build upon theory from the disciplines of management, engineering, physics, systems theory, organizational theory, and other applied areas of inquiry. Theory can be borrowed from a variety of other disciplines, grounded in library and information practice, and rearticulated for application in the library and information professions.

Assessing the information needs of individuals and groups is fundamental to customized library and information services. In this chapter, the service cycle was defined and methods for collecting information for a needs assessment have been outlined. The Community Analysis Research Institute (CARI) Model has been introduced and defined, and the importance of theory in understanding needs assessment results has been discussed.

REFERENCES

Glazier, Jack D., and Robert Grover. 2002. "A multidisciplinary framework for theory building." *Library Trends* 50: 317–332

Greer, Roger C. 1987. A model for the discipline of information science. In *Intellectual foundations for information professionals*, ed. Herbert K. Achleitner, 3–25. Boulder, CO: Social Science Monographs; New York: Distributed by Columbia University Press.

Greer, Roger C., Robert J. Grover, and Susan G. Fowler. 2007. *Introduction to the library and information professions*. Westport, CT & London: Libraries Unlimited.

Greer, Roger C., and Martha L. Hale. 1982. The community analysis process. In *Public librarianship: a reader*, ed. J. Robbins-Carter, 358–366. Littleton, CO: Libraries Unlimited.

Kuhlthau, Carol C. 2004. *Seeking meaning: a process approach to library and information services*. Westport, CT: Libraries Unlimited.

Lincoln, Y. S. and E. G. Guba. 1985. *Naturalistic inquiry*. Beverly Hills, CA: Sage Publications.

Schneider, Georg. 1961. *Theory and history of bibliography*. Trans. by Ralph Robert Shaw. New York: Scarecrow Press.

CHAPTER 5

Gathering Data
for Decision-Making

CHAPTER OVERVIEW

Both qualitative and quantitative data-gathering methods can be used effectively to assess community information needs. The literature of reading research and library user needs is reviewed. Methods of data-gathering are outlined, along with suggestions for using surveys and when not to. A rationale for using intuitive and impressionistic data is presented. Use of the Internet and library registration information is discussed as sources for community information.

READER STUDIES

During the 1920s and 1930s faculty at the University of Chicago conducted a number of extensive reading studies in an effort to document the impact of reading on the general population and improve the level of library services. Impetus for the study of reading interests was provided by the Committee on the Reading Interests and Habits of Adults, appointed jointly by the American Library Association and the American Association for Adult Education (Waples and Tyler 1931, xviii). The Committee commissioned the assembly of studies already completed; these results by Gray and Monroe (1929) suggested that adult reading is an issue that can best be addressed by studying groups of adults. Leaders in the research effort to analyze adult reading in more detail, with implications for library services, were Douglas Waples (1932, 1940) and Leon Carnovsky (1939, 1940).

Waples and Tyler's (1931) extensive study defined what adults would like to read. The researchers identified groups by amount of schooling, occupation, and type of environment. Reading preferences were defined by topics of periodical articles written in contemporary magazines during a ten-year period. These 117 headings were used to categorize the reading preferences of adult readers. This study confirmed the relevance of studying social groups in order to determine patterns of use.

These and other reader studies led to the determination that readers' choices were strongly influenced by readers' "predispositions," which include " ... the reader's sympathies with the various groups in which he is placed by his sex, age, income, education, and other traits—sympathies which combine to sway the reader toward or away from the direction in which the publication is slanted ... " (Waples, Berelson, and Bradshaw 1940, 8). These studies also recognized the unique preferences of individuals. This early research preceded studies in psychology and education that revealed a variety of learning styles that contribute significantly to information search strategies and to one's interests in reading, viewing, and listening.

While they were informative, and served as a foundation for further studies, the reading studies were focused narrowly on reading preferences and did not address the broader concept of information needs. This broader issue is addressed later and in more depth, as discussed below.

STUDIES OF INFORMATION NEEDS

Determining the information needs of clientele in order to plan and provide information services has been a concern of library and information professionals since Melvil Dewey first challenged librarians to know the library's users: "He [the librarian] must see that his library contains, as far as possible, the best books on the best subjects, regarding carefully the wants of his special community" (Dewey 1976, 22).

Numerous quantitative studies of library users have been conducted (for example, D'Elia and Rodger 1991, 1994, 1996). Studies of users can be very helpful in a planning process, as D'Elia, Rodger, and Williams (1991) demonstrated with a user study of the St. Paul (Minnesota) Public Library. Group interviews and a system-wide patron survey broadened the perspectives of key decision makers and enriched the body of information available for making decisions. The study was helpful in identifying user roles and the services needed to support those roles.

Such user studies are informative to the administration of a library because the user patterns can be discerned; however, the community's information needs, including the needs of non-users, are not measured.

Wilson (1981) noted the confusion in the research literature related to information use studies and the use of the term "information need." He investigated the literature of psychology and listed the three categories for human needs, as determined by that field of study:

- physiological needs, such as the need for food, water, shelter, etc.;
- affective needs (sometimes called psychological or emotional needs) such as the need for attainment, for domination, etc.;
- and cognitive needs, such as the need to plan, to learn, etc. (Wilson 1981, 7)

Wilson also posited that an information need might be prompted by other factors as well:

Many factors other than the existence of a need will play a part: the importance of satisfying the need, the penalty incurred by acting in the absence of full information, the availability of information sources and the costs of using them, and so forth. Many decisions are taken with incomplete information or on the basis of beliefs, whether we call these prejudices, faith or ideology. So, information-seeking may not occur at all, or there may be a time delay between the recognition of the need and the information seeking acts; or, in the case of affective needs, neither the need nor its satisfaction may be consciously recognized by the actor; or a cognitive need of fairly low salience may be satisfied by chance days, months, or even years after it has been recognized, or the availability of the information may bring about the recognition of a previously unrecognized cognitive need. (Wilson 1981, 8)

Wilson also noted that cognitive or affective information needs may be prompted by an individual's roles in life, including social roles (e.g., parent, homeowner, voter) as well as occupational or work-related roles: "So far as specialized information systems are concerned, the most relevant of these roles in 'work role', that is, the set of activities, responsibilities etc. of an individual, usually in some organizational setting, in pursuit of earnings and other satisfactions" (Wilson 1981, 9).

Another issue which has been raised by Siatri (1999) in his review of user studies, is that "information need" is sometimes confused with "wants" and "requests," and information need studies have been confused with information user studies. Siatri's review of user studies documented myriad user studies that have been done on identified groups of users.

Siatri (1999, 133–134) identified numerous studies of information users in the hard sciences, including the fields of biochemistry, medicine, engineering, and physics, during the 1950s and 1960s. In the 1960s, the number of user studies increased, the studies became more sophisticated, and they expanded the user groups to the social and behavioral sciences (Siatri 1999, 134–135). An important development noted by Siatri (1999) was the establishment of the Centre for Research on User Studies at Sheffield University in 1975. This center conducted research on a variety of subjects and provided seminars and training courses in research methods and published papers on the research.

An important community study during this period was the Warner et al. (1973) study of Baltimore citizens' information needs (Siatri 1999, 136). This study sought to identify information needs of 1,615 households through interviews.

Less prominent in the professional literature is research on information needs of communities that can benefit library and information professionals who serve large, diverse populations. Furthermore, there is a need for practical research methodologies, data-gathering techniques that can be applied within a professional setting by busy professionals who need accurate information for planning and implementing information services.

Knowing the needs of clientele can be determined by competent staff members who interact regularly with clientele. As in customer-oriented retail businesses, library staff can routinely ask clientele if they have found what they wanted. As Wallace (2007, 126) suggested, "Front-line employees should share information gleaned from customer contact with other library employees, including those who have little contact with external customers." Wallace remarked that numerous collection-related data sources can help identify the current information needs of library users, as listed below:

- individual item circulation statistics
- in-library use counts
- reserve lists
- purchase requests
- interlibrary loan data
- reference or readers' advisory question data, including information on unanswered questions
- comparisons with competitors, for example by using a tool such as OCLC's WorldCat Collection Analysis (Wallace 2007, 127)

While analysis of such customer relations helps determine the information needs of clientele who use the library, what about those clientele who do not use the library? How do we determine their needs?

Environmental Scanning

"Environmental scanning" is a term used primarily in the business community, but that also applies in studies of library users' information needs. An early study by Aguilar (1967, 1) introduced the concept with this statement: "Any high-level executive worth his salt spends a great deal of time scanning the business environment, whether he realizes it or not." Aguilar commented that "scanning" is the acquiring of information and further defined "environmental scanning" as " ... scanning for information about events and relationships in a company's outside environment, the knowledge of which would assist top management in its task of charting the company's future course of action." (Aguilar 1967, 1). A study of 20 corporations in the United States by Bourgeois (1995) identified environmental scanning as the first of five key steps for informing the strategies in these companies:

1. environmental scanning
2. objective setting
3. competitive weapons selection
4. power distribution
5. resource allocation

The purpose of environmental scanning, looking at outside environmental variables, is to enable decision makers to improve strategic planning and decision-making. The implication is that such scanning of the environment will also improve decisions and planning for the short term as well.

Aguilar's (1967) study of large and small corporations concluded that strategic information was being gathered, but a substantial amount was wasted. A major reason for ineffective use of information, which he described as "fractionalization" of the organization's scanning activities. This problem was manifested by (1) the failure of units and individuals to gather accessible information that was important for their organization, and (2) the failure of company leaders to receive relevant information already available in the company (Aguilar 1967, 184). In other words, external information of value to an organization may already be available, but it may be "squandered" through an ineffective communication system within the organization. Internal organization and communication is addressed in Chapter 13 of this book.

Aguilar's (1967) field study included 137 managers from 41 companies located in the United States and Western Europe. The companies studied included 25 chemical manufacturing companies, one pharmaceutical company, seven non-chemical manufacturing companies, and eight service companies dealing with the chemical industry (Aguilar 1967, 209–210). Aguilar concluded that environmental scanning activities varied little from industry to industry (p. 37). The major topics identified as important information sources by managers were grouped as follows:

- **Market tidings.** Current activities in the market and competitive field, including market potential, competitors, pricing, and customers
- **Technical tidings.** Technology and new processes, product problems, costs, and licensing
- **Broad issues.** Events outside the industrial environment, including political and national events and governmental decisions and policies

- **Acquisition leads.** Leads for joint ventures, acquisitions, and mergers
- **Other tidings.** Miscellaneous components, including suppliers, resources, and available staff.

The most important of these topics, as indicated by the responses of managers, were market tidings (accounting for 58% of all responses), followed by technology (accounting for 18% of responses). In other words, market activities and technology accounted for 76 percent of the environmental information required by managers.

Costa's (1999) review of environmental scanning literature attested that subsequent studies reinforce Aguilar's (1967) views of the importance of environmental scanning, and Costa declares that the majority of authors in the literature of environmental scanning agree that the main functions of scanning are:

- to learn about events and trends in the external environment;
- to establish relationships between events and trends;
- to make sense of the data;
- and to extract the main implications for decision-making and strategy development (Costa 1999, 5)

The business literature seems to be in agreement that marketplace information is critical for informed decision-making, regardless of the age or size of a company. Mohan-Neill (1995) conducted research that suggested that new and smaller ventures are less likely to engage in formal or structured marketing research activities, and are less informed about their environment than older and larger firms. Despite the value of environmental scanning for making decisions and planning, Costa (1999, 5) declared that this information-gathering technique is not in widespread use in businesses.

According to Costa (1999, 5–6), the elements most commonly identified during environmental scanning are political, economic, social, and technological—known as PEST analysis. Costa (1999, 6) notes that the data collection in organizations is "irregular, periodic, or continuous in increasing order of sophistication and complexity." Costa (1999) further notes that irregular systems are usually reactive in their planning, and periodic systems are more sophisticated and complex in their approach to problem solving. Continuous systems are the ideal, because their aim is to find opportunity and take a proactive stance in planning the growth of an organization.

An example of a systematic approach to environmental scanning was produced by Aaker (1983), whose Strategic Information Scanning System (SISS) identified six action steps:

1. Specify information needs
2. Specify information sources

3. Identify participants
4. Assign scanning tasks
5. Store and process information
6. Disseminate information

This model is useful as a guide for the process, but it lacks the specific processes for library and information agencies to adapt the framework for gathering external information. However, the implication for libraries and information agencies is that environmental scanning, focusing on both users and potential users, should play a substantial role in the planning and decision-making process. The impact of users and technology should be a major consideration in the planning process.

Community Analysis

While environmental scanning is a business practice, a similar study of an environment to discover information needs is a "community analysis." As noted in Chapter 2, Greer and Hale (1982) defined "community analysis" as follows:

Community analysis is a systematic process of collecting, organizing and analyzing data about the library and its environment. It is designed to assist the administrator in choosing from among alternative patterns of satisfying residents' information needs and interests. (p. 358)

More recently, Westbrook (2001) used the terminology "community information-needs analysis" (CINA), defined as follows:

A community information-needs analysis (CINA) is a structured, planned, formal study that identifies the information requirements of the people within a library's jurisdiction. (p. 2)

Westbrook further defined the community as that prescribed in the library's mission statement, and she indicates what a CINA is *not*: "Most important, it is not a study of what current users are currently doing. A CINA looks at what users and potential users *need*, rather than what current users actually do" (Westbrook 2001, 3).

Westbrook's (2001) methods incorporate a number of data-gathering techniques, including interviews, focus groups, unobtrusive observations, obtrusive observations, mailed questionnaires, e-mailed questionnaires, web-based questionnaires, the Delphi technique, and diaries, journals, and logs. Westbrook (2001) also incorporates a number of in-house data to assess user information needs—information gleaned from circulation and interlibrary records, reference statistics, online search transaction logs, remote site use information, programming attendance records, and instruction activity reports.

The authors of this book note that the methods proposed by Westbrook are valid and are acceptable formal or scientific methods for conducting research; however, we believe that there are additional systematic data-collection techniques that are informative, useful, readily available, and easily incorporated into community needs assessments.

Information Use Studies

As noted earlier, environmental scans, while recognized as valuable means for providing information for decision-making and planning, are often ignored, especially by small organizations. Likewise, libraries and other information agencies often neglect to conduct information use studies or community analysis because of the "crush" of daily professional duties. As Plosker (2002, 64) wrote, " … user surveys tend to 'slide off the plate' as information professionals go about their busy schedules." Given the increased use of remote library use through the Internet, Plosker cites the decline in the face-to-face use of reference services as a solid rationale for conducting a user survey or audit. Plosker (2002) recommends the following strategies for exploring the changing needs of users:

- The traditional reference interview can probe users' interests in extending user services.
- Joining project and/or community teams enables information professionals to understand various constituencies' goals and interests.
- In academic or public libraries, users can be segmented by academic discipline, or by grade or age level.
- A survey by mail, e-mail, or through an appropriate newsletter can be conducted.
- Recent internal correspondence, patron communications, and library publications can be examined for trends or themes.
- A verbal survey can be conducted by telephone.

Information use patterns are changing in step with the changing information environment and the proliferation of online and other electronic information sources. Tenopir's (2003) analysis of 200 studies of users' interaction with online information resources revealed the following common conclusions:

- Faculty and students like electronic resources and adopt them readily if they perceive the sources to be convenient to use.
- Experts in different disciplines have different use patterns and preferences for format.

- Print is still a part of research in nearly every discipline.
- Personal subscriptions to journals are decreasing in favor of electronic journal subscriptions provided by the library.
- High school and college students use the Internet more than the library.
- There is much diversity in the use of information resources—no preferred use pattern or no typical user.

Because of this diversity and because of individual preferences, it is vital in this changing information environment for information professionals to continuously conduct assessments of the information needs of individuals and groups.

One way of monitoring the changing needs of groups is the formation of "market councils" as described by Forrest (2005). In order to introduce a formal mechanism for segmenting and determining the needs of its user community, the General Libraries at Emory University created market councils for humanities, social science, science, international and area studies, business, and undergraduates. This approach has been successful " ... as an effective means for ensuring that the library's information resources, internal processes and service initiatives are continually responsive to the changing needs of Emory's academic community" (Forrest 2005, 7).

The Use of Qualitative Research Methods and Intuition

Qualitative research methods have evolved in answer to the complexity of today's world and the necessity to study complex social problems. The following points are implications for research drawn from Lincoln and Guba (1985, 141–156).

- Research must be conducted in a natural setting, diminishing the possibility that the controlling of variables in an experimental study could influence results of a research project. A problem must be studied in its context in order to be fully understood.
- Researchers must be satisfied with an emergent research design. Because of the complexity of societal problems, it is not possible to design in advance a complex research design that will enable collection of data to address a problem. People are unpredictable, and researchers must allow sufficient flexibility in the research design to allow the scope of the problem to unfold unpredictably.
- The human is a plausible research-gathering instrument who can understand the emotional, or irrational, elements of a problem.
- Qualitative methods of data-gathering are most appropriate for accommodating complex social issues involving multiple, sometimes

conflicting, realities. Such methods include interviews, observations, content analysis, and various unobtrusive measures. Qualitative measures are also very useful in social problems, for which little is known.

- Utilization of tacit knowledge, including impressions and intuition. Data-gathering may include data collected through the recognition of nonverbal cues or in response to "hunches" or a "gut reaction." These intuitive responses, part of the holistic approach to problem solving, may lead to the discovery of new relationships, resulting in new theory. A more detailed discussion of this is found below.
- Data analysis is usually accomplished by inductive reasoning. Use of qualitative methods results in the collection of large quantities of rich data. By pouring over the data, trends and relationships tend to emerge through inductive analysis, resulting in discoveries which had not been anticipated.
- Purposive or theoretical sampling replaces random samples in research projects. In-depth study of a small sample, using qualitative methods, requires a sample that is representative of the special population under study. The sample is selected specifically to represent the problem under study.
- Boundaries for the study are determined by the problem under investigation. Because there are no hypotheses to provide limitations for data collection, the nature of the problem, the subjects, and limitations on the time, resources, and energy of the researcher will impose boundaries on the study.
- The application of findings must be done tentatively. Because of the limited scope of a study, a small purposive sample, and contextual nature of the inquiry, the generalizability of results must be carefully and tentatively considered. Generalizations are best applied in numerous contexts, with the theory restated and refined in order to fit the definitions imposed by the new context.
- The case study takes on new importance. Careful and detailed description of a context for purpose of analysis results in a thoroughly implemented case study that provides the circumstances for participants to react to the context of their environment. The case study method is an important vehicle for gaining the understanding required for theory building.

For a more complete analysis of qualitative methods, see Grover and Glazier (1985) and Glazier (1985).

The Use of Intuition

What data-gathering methods should be used in collecting data for a community analysis? Hale (1986) articulated a continuum of data-gathering

Figure 5.1   Data-gathering Methods.

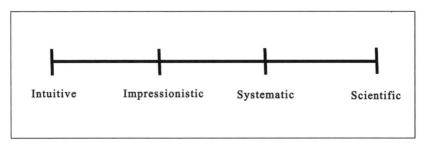

methods that can be applied to the assessment of information needs. Hale described a range of techniques which include (1) common sense or intuitive, (2) impressionistic, (3) systematic, and (4) scientific. That model is found in Figure 5.1.

This continuum of data-gathering begins with the intuitive data-gathering that we carry out continuously. Over the years we collect data through our senses, hearing and seeing myriad events daily. Through all of our learning, we develop "hunches" or a "gut feeling" when posed a question or queried about a relationship. Without further attempts to gather data, we may articulate our hunch, for example, that a particular clientele tends to use certain kinds of information sources.

Impressions

A second type of data gathering is impressionistic; the impressions we receive when we walk around, listen, and observe what is going on around us. Impressionistic data are gathered in a library, for example, by walking around the facility and observing and listening to the library users. Likewise, we can drive around a community or walk around a school to gain impressions of that community and its lifestyle or culture. Impressionistic data gathering is intentional but not systematic. Included among impressionistic methods are the following:

- **Scanning.** A quick but thorough look at a problem.
- **Brainstorming.** A group participating in sharing their impressions related to a problem or area of study.
- **Product approaches.** Impressions of needed information services or products and the information professional's knowledge of how to create that product.
- **Walk-arounds or drive-arounds.** Scanning of an environment (local community, school, college, or corporate enterprise) by walking or driving around to observe.

Systematic Data-gathering

A third type of data-gathering is a systematic gathering of data for a purpose. Much of the community analysis model which we will discuss in later chapters is a systematic approach to gathering data found in existing sources: censuses, circulation records of a library, newspaper stories, web sites, and other such information sources. Systematic techniques are planned more carefully than impressionistic data gathering; consequently, they are more reliable and more generalizable than intuitive or impressionistic approaches.

By controlling the use of systematic methods, these methods may be considered scientific. For example, Hale (1986) discusses observation and "asking" as two systematic methods, but both may be considered scientific when more carefully structured and controlled in gathering data.

Scientific Research

The most familiar method for data-gathering is scientific research, the formal data-gathering that researchers do when conducting a formal study. Scientific methods are the experimental, historical, survey, and structured observational methods usually applied in a formal study by professionals, researchers, or students. These are the methods usually used in action research—studies of professional problems done on the job by practicing professionals. The methodologies are carefully considered for the research problem, and appropriate data-gathering methods are selected and rigorously applied so that all of the conventions of research are followed, providing results that will contribute to the body of knowledge of the profession.

Scientific research conforms to the accepted conventions of a discipline or profession, and includes the qualitative methods mentioned above, along with quantitative measures such as questionnaires, interviews, and experimental studies. Qualitative methods, once considered unscientific, are generally accepted in formal studies related to library and information studies.

Because scientific methods are so exacting and expensive to accomplish, the authors consider them impractical for use in conducting a community needs analysis. Data collected during a community analysis are used for management decision-making, and the expense of conducting a scientific study is unwarranted. We recommend intuitive, impressionistic, or systematic data gathering techniques as a more practical but effective way to collect data for a community needs assessment. In other words, we suggest using data that already exist; when additional information is required, we suggest methods that are easy to carry out and information that is collected through intuition, impressions, and systematic data-gathering.

WHEN TO USE SURVEYS—AND WHEN NOT TO

When "information needs analysis" is mentioned, most professionals immediately think of a survey. A survey is described by Powell (1997, 57) as:

a group of research methodologies commonly used to determine the present status of a given phenomenon. The basic assumption of most survey research is that, by carefully following certain scientific procedures, one can make inferences about a large group of elements by studying a relatively small number selected from the larger group.

Indeed, questionnaires are appropriate for uses in certain situations, and they are a waste of time in others. In this section, we explore the possibilities and problems associated with questionnaires or written surveys.

Surveys are useful when little is known of a population, and it is necessary to describe a population in general terms. Adams and Beck (1995, 2) reported that libraries at a majority of colleges use surveys as a way of determining what users think about library services and facilities and identifying users' priorities. Their 1995 survey of 214 college and small university library directors revealed that 70 percent of the respondents had conducted at least one survey on library use in the last five years (Adams and Beck 1995, 3). Most of the surveys (90%) were written surveys in a written questionnaire format. Focus groups and interviews were the other methods used. Both non-surveying and surveying libraries responded to a large degree (60% and 74%, respectively) that the most frequent reason for not conducting surveys was lack of available staff time, and nearly two-thirds (65%) of non-surveying libraries named lack of funding to be a constraint (p. 4).

Surveys can reach a large audience and can glean a great deal of relevant information, but creating a sample which is generalizable to the population as a whole is labor-intensive and, we believe, impractical for libraries and information agencies with staff who are not trained researchers. In addition, there are software packages that enable fast turnaround, and the analysis is all done electronically. Zoomerang (http://info.zoomerang.com/) is an example of such a software instrument.

Written Questionnaires

Powell (1997, 90–91) lists several advantages of the written questionnaire, and these advantages apply to e-mail surveys as well. The questionnaire encourages frank answers because the researcher can guarantee anonymity.

1. There is less likelihood of interviewer bias.
2. The fixed format of the questionnaire eliminates variation in the questioning process.

3. The questionnaire can be completed at the convenience of the respondent, encouraging thoughtful answers.
4. Questionnaires can be constructed to permit relatively easy collection and analysis of data.
5. Large amounts of data can be collected in a short period.
6. Questionnaires are relatively inexpensive to administer.

Of course, negative features are also in evidence, as Powell (1997, 91–92) enumerates:

1. A questionnaire eliminates personal contact between the subject and the researcher, although one may argue that lack of contact minimizes researcher bias (advantage #1, above).
2. The respondent is not able to qualify answers or ask for clarification of ambiguous questions.
3. Persons who are highly opinionated are more likely to respond to a questionnaire, increasing the likelihood of a biased sample.
4. Questionnaires may be more difficult for uneducated respondents to complete, decreasing the likelihood that they will respond, possibly resulting in a biased return.
5. There seems to be a resistance to questionnaires, sometimes causing respondents to "sabotage" their responses.

Additionally, we the authors are concerned that the data collected in this manner may not be generalizable and useful for making management decisions.

Interviews

Powell (1997, 112–113) credits telephone or in-person interviews with the following advantages over written questionnaires:

1. The response rate is nearly always better than that of a written questionnaire, permitting a sample more representative of the population studied.
2. The personal contact encourages subjects to respond fully.
3. Because of the personal contact, an interview may have more questions than a written questionnaire.
4. The personal contact enables the subject to clarify ambiguous questions.
5. The interview is generally more likely to provide responses for issues that are more personal, complex, or value-laden.

Focus Groups

A "focus group" is a group interview, and the group can be selected to represent the dimensions of the population studied. For example, a college faculty focus group might include faculty members who can provide the perspectives of faculty members in the sciences, humanities, fine arts, social sciences, and professional schools. The composition of the focus group should reflect the objectives of the study and represent the population being studied.

Powell (1997, 113–114) cited the following advantages of focus groups:

1. These groups can benefit from the interchange among group members.
2. The interviews can be conducted in a relatively short time span.
3. People in a group tend to be less inhibited than individuals.

On the other hand, focus groups may not be representative of the population, biased conclusions may result, and the results may be difficult to quantify. In addition, the moderator must be skilled enough to guide the discussion, but to do so in a manner that will not lead the group in a direction that will result in bias. Results are usually recorded for later analysis.

When *Not* to Use Surveys

Survey techniques are useful when little is known of a population and there is a need to gather information rather quickly. Depending on the objectives of the survey, any one of the techniques, or a combination, described above can be used to effectively gather baseline or initial information. For example, a written questionnaire might be a good initial attempt to gather information, and the results can be used as a springboard for interviews or focus groups designed to probe more deeply into the findings of the initial questionnaire.

Surveys are *not* the beginning and the end of a community needs assessment. Surveys are a set of tools that can be used in conjunction with other data, as described later in this book, if surveys are to be used at all. Because survey techniques are structured and require a degree of expertise and a substantial investment of time and resources, we suggest that surveys are most appropriate to use when the other systematic data-gathering methods may not produce the information needed to make decisions for providing information services. Referring to the Hale continuum described earlier in the chapter, we recommend intuitive, impressionistic, and systematic data-gathering, using scientific methods only when additional and more precise information is required.

USING THE INTERNET TO GATHER COMMUNITY INFORMATION

The Internet is a relatively new electronic tool that can be used to gather information about a community. As noted earlier, software is available to conduct written questionnaires via e-mail and web sites. The Internet can be a fast means for communicating with individuals or groups who may or may not be library users. In addition, local web sites can be useful for studying the characteristics of a community by browsing and checking for characteristics of individuals, agencies, and groups as they appear on their web sites. This form of information gathering will be discussed further in the chapters that follow, and we provide examples in our case study.

USING REGISTRATION DATA

For information professionals working in a library or other type of information service agency, the registration files of individual users provide a great deal of information regarding the individuals and groups that are using the agency's services. Whether these records are paper or electronic, they can be mined to determine the heavy users and their preferences for topics and formats of information resources. The user registration database holds a wealth of user information that is often ignored, except to identify and retrieve overdue items. Information from the registration database will be discussed in the following chapters.

SUMMARY

This chapter has investigated the efforts that have been made in the library and information profession to identify the needs of library users and their reading preferences. The complexity of this task also has been explored, as well as the information-seeking behavior of individuals and groups that have been studied by numerous researchers and practitioners in the library and information profession. The roles of individuals and groups have been identified as a key variable in studying information needs. The field of business has developed and applied environmental scanning techniques to determine attributes of the external environment in which a business exists so that the needs of customers can be determined as an enterprise plans for the future. Similarly, in the library field, community information needs analysis (CINA) explores both the external and internal environments of the library or information agency in order to revise, plan, and customize information services. A variety of data-gathering techniques have been explored for use in conducting a community needs assessment, and a data-gathering continuum which incorporates intuitive, impressionistic, systematic, and scientific data-gathering was described.

While survey techniques can be useful to gather information for a community needs assessment, the authors suggest using intuitive, impressionistic, and systematic data gathering in professional settings due to the commitment of time and resources required for scientific data-gathering. The application of data-gathering techniques, using existing resources, will be the focus of the chapters that follow.

REFERENCES

Adams, Mignon S. and Jeffrey A. Beck. 1995. *User surveys in college libraries*. CLIP Note #23. Chicago: Association of College and Research Libraries, a Division of the American Library Association.

Aguilar, Francis Joseph. 1967. *Scanning the business environment*. New York and London: Macmillan.

Bourgeois, L. J. III, "Strategy making, environment, and economic performance: a conceptual and empirical exploration," doctoral dissertation, University Microfilms International in Costa, Jorge. 1995. An empirically-based review of the concept of environmental scanning. *International Journal of Contemporary Hospitality Management*, 7, 7, 4–9.

Carnovsky, Leon. 1934. A study of the relationship between reading interest and actual reading. *Library Quarterly*, 4, 1, 76–110.

Costa, Jorge. 1995. An empirically-based review of the concept of environmental scanning. *International Journal of Contemporary Hospitality Management*, 7, 7, 4–9.

D'Elia, George and Eleanor Jo Rodger. 1991. *Free Library of Philadelphia patron survey: Final report*. University of Minnesota Center for Survey Research.

———. 1994. Public library roles and patron use: Why patrons use the library. *Public Libraries*, 33, 135–44.

———. 1996. Customer satisfaction with public libraries. *Public Libraries*, 35, 292–7.

Dewey, Melvil. 1976. The profession. In *Landmarks of library literature 1876–1976*, ed. Dianne J. Ellsworth and Norman D. Stevens, 21–23. Metuchen, NJ: Scarecrow Press.

Forrest, Charles. 2005. Segmenting the library market, reaching out to the user community by reaching across the organization. *Georgia Library Quarterly* 42, 1, 4–7.

Gray, William S. and Ruth Monroe. 1929. *The reading interests and habits of adults*. New York: Macmillan.

Greer, Roger C. and Martha L. Hale. 1982. The community analysis process. In *Public librarianship: A reader*, ed. J. Robbins-Carter, 358–366. Littleton, CO: Libraries Unlimited.

Hale, Martha. L. 1986. Administrators and information: a review of methodologies used for diagnosing information use. In *Advances in Librarianship*, Volume 14, ed. W. Simonton, 75–99. Orlando, FL: Academic Press.

Mohan-Neill, Sumaria Indra. 1995. The influence of firm's age and size on its environmental scanning activities. *Journal of Small Business Management* 33, 4, 10–21.

Plosker, George R. Sept./Oct. 2002. Conducting user surveys: An ongoing information imperative. *Online* 26, 5, 64–68.

Powell, Ronald R. 1997. *Basic research methods for librarians*. 3rd ed. Greenwich, CT and London: Ablex Publishing Corp.

Siatri, Rania. 1999. The evolution of user studies. *Libri* 49, 132–141.

Tenopir, Carol. 2003. What user studies tell us. *Library Journal* 128, 14 (September 1, 2003):32.

Wallace, Karen. 2007. Marketing mindset: Focusing on the customer, from technical services to circulation. *Feliciter* 3, 126–129.

Waples, Douglas. n.d. *People and print; social aspects of reading in the depression*. Chicago: The University of Chicago Press.

———. 1932. The relation of subject interests to actual reading. *Library Quarterly*, 2, 1, 42–70.

Waples, Douglas, Bernard Berelson, and Franklyn R. Bradshaw. 1940. *What reading does to people*. Chicago: The University of Chicago Press.

Waples, Douglas and Leon Carnovsky. 1939. *Libraries and readers in the State of New York*. Chicago: The University of Chicago Press.

Warner, E. S., A. D. Murray, and V. E. Palmour. 1973. Information needs of urban residents. U.S. Department of Health, Education and Welfare, Office of Education, Bureau of Libraries and Learning Resources. Cited in Siatri (1999, 136).

Westbrook, Lynn. 2001. *Identifying and analyzing user needs; a complete handbook and ready-to-use assessment handbook with disk*. New York and London: Neal-Schuman Publishers.

Wilson, T. D. 1981. On user studies and information needs. *The Journal of Documentation* 37, 1, 3–15.

Zoomerang. http://info.zoomerang.com/ (accessed February 28, 2010).

CHAPTER 6

The Information Needs of Individuals

CHAPTER OVERVIEW

Our model for collecting data for a community analysis entails an examination of a community from four perspectives: individuals, groups, agencies, and lifestyles. This chapter focuses on individuals. It begins with a definition of individuals and an overview of principles associated with information psychology, the study of how individuals process and use information. These principles are important to apply as data are gathered and services are planned for the individual user. Sources of information about individuals in a community are suggested, including library registration files and government data sources available on the Internet.

DEFINITION OF INDIVIDUALS

In Chapter 4 we noted that this perspective of community analysis requires assessing needs through the demographics of a community. These demographics present a composite view of the individuals in a service area. Here is an important point: Be certain that the service area of the information agency is clearly identified. Often, the defined service area and political boundaries used to define census tracts are not congruent. Thus, gathering demographic data from the census may not provide an accurate reading of individuals served by the information agency.

Including pertinent census data results in an analysis of such variables as the population of the municipality, the ethnic makeup, and its socioeconomic makeup. The following are characteristics that are informative in the analysis:

- Age grouping characteristics
- Family structure, including households and children, marital status
- Education characteristics, including school enrollment and years of school completed
- Economic characteristics, including employment status, occupation, industry, commuting time and distance, and income

The examples above for municipalities can be adapted easily to other kinds of communities as well. The communities of colleges, schools, private enterprises, and government agencies also can be analyzed in the same way. For example, a school librarian would pay attention to the number of faculty and students, the size of academic departments, and the ethnic composition of the student body. Likewise, the school librarian should pay attention to the demographics of the community as an influence on the school system. All of the elements of a community analysis for a municipality could be considered, but in less depth. The school librarian would look for indicators that support the needs of the students and teachers.

Academic communities should look at data similar to that of schools: the numbers of students in each department, the schools and colleges within the university, the number of majors and minors, and other distinguishing characteristics of the student body and faculty. What makes the college or university unique? How does this uniqueness influence library and information services?

In many types of special libraries, the information professional works alone or with a small cadre of professionals and technical staff within a much larger organization that is supported by the library. For example, a law library within a government agency or law firm is staffed by information professionals with both knowledge of the law and expertise in library and information resources and services. The clientele may include attorneys, judges, law students, paralegals, and perhaps the general public.

Regardless of the type of community, analysis of **individuals** is intended to break down a complex organization to look at the people who make up that organization. That is the purpose of analyzing the demographics of a community.

When studying the individuals in a community, the following questions should be considered:

- Who are the usual library/information users? Where are they?
- What are the occupations or job categories of the community?
- Who are the non-users of the library and information services?
- What variables account for non-use of library/information services?
- What has been the rate of growth or loss of population?
- Are there areas with special characteristics? What are they?

This information can be found readily in existing agencies, e.g., the community library, the city planning agency, school offices, local chambers of commerce, zoning boards, utility companies, and public agency web sites.

Colleges and universities would have some of this information in administrative offices at the college/university or at the system level. Special library agencies would also house some of this information in the administrative offices.

PRINCIPLES OF INFORMATION PSYCHOLOGY

The goal of information professionals is to create and operate information systems and services that meet the information needs of a specific client population. This goal of customizing information service requires knowledge of human behavior associated with the acquisition and use of information. "Information psychology" is the term we use to identify the field of information science concerned with the development and study of this theory of human behavior. Information psychology employs behavioral theory to the library and information professions in the same way that educational psychology applies principles of psychology to the education profession.

Knowledge of information psychology is required for a library and information professional in order to design and implement an information service that addresses the information needs and preferences of individuals. Consequently, we will now investigate briefly the characteristics of information psychology as a background for studying the characteristics and information needs of individuals in a community.

Behavioral Processes of Information Psychology

The field of information psychology addresses the following questions:

1. How does a person decide that he or she has a need for information? What are the conditions or motives that provoke this awareness?
2. What processes are involved in decisions to satisfy or ignore the need?
3. What strategies are employed in searching for information, and how do these strategies differ among individuals?
4. What are the variations in behaviors associated with the search for information? How does the configuration of the use of a particular information system affect these behaviors?
5. How does the medium of the information (book, electronic publication, video, etc.) influence the individual's selection and use of the information?

6. What methods and criteria are employed in evaluating the relevance of information acquired?
7. What are the behaviors associated with the processes of assimilating information? How does information become knowledge? How does format and system design affect this aspect of behavior?
8. What cognitive styles are employed in information processing? How does learning style influence information searching, information retrieval, and information use?
9. How do individuals organize, store, and retrieve information from memory?
10. What are the varieties of forms and patterns of information utilization? (Greer, Grover, and Fowler 2007, 50–51)

Theory Supporting Information Psychology

Contributing to an understanding of these questions are the research and theory from the following fields:

1. Behavioral psychology, including personality theory, perception theory, motivation theory, attitude theory, cognitive science, theories of intelligence, role theory, and learning theory
2. Psycho-linguistics
3. Physiology
4. Religion
5. Educational psychology
6. Social psychology
7. Sociology of information
8. Information engineering
9. Information organization management (Greer, Grover, and Fowler 2007, 51)

An important aspect of information psychology is an understanding of an individual's roles. As noted above, role theory contributes to an understanding of the information user's needs. Role theory, a subdiscipline of psychology, is the study of the activity of people in groups. In groups, individuals engage in expected behaviors and take certain actions and positions. These actions and positions define a role. Each role of an individual suggests information needs. The role of parent, for example, suggests a need for information about children, their health, diet, recreation, education, and other aspects of child rearing. Likewise, professional or occupational roles imply other needs that foster an individual's needs for work-related information.

The Environmental Context for Information Psychology

The behavioral processes outlined above are influenced by variables external to the practice of the library and information professions. We call these variables "the environmental and social context." These variables apply to all aspects of information work, whether working with individuals or groups (Greer, Grover, and Fowler 2007, 53–57).

1. Culture: language, philosophical and moral values, educational system, concept of time, historical background, and all features which comprise a community's culture
2. Physical geography: aspects such as climate and topographical characteristics
3. Political structure of society: the system for governance and under-lying values regarding the role of government in a dynamic society
4. Legislation and regulations issued by legislative and regulatory agencies of government
5. The economic system under which the culture functions
6. Technology: the level of sophistication in terms of computer and telecommunication technology
7. Information policy: copyright laws, policies regarding secrecy, censorship, privacy, ownership, the public's right to know, and a government's responsibility to inform

The needs and uses of information by individuals and groups are influenced by the policy and environmental variables in the community as the culture varies. The community culture we refer to in this book as "lifestyles," a concept which is discussed in Chapter 9. Examples of each environmental context variable are found in Greer, Grover, and Fowler (2007, 54–57).

LOCATING DATA FOR INDIVIDUALS

Now that we have defined what we mean by individuals and have provided a framework for thinking about individuals and the ways in which they process information, let us examine the ways in which we can collect data about individuals, using existing information sources. We will examine library records, census data, and other data that are readily available in our communities.

Library Registration Files

The first place to begin answering the questions listed above is within the library or information agency itself. Registration files can be searched to determine who the users are and where they live. From registration and circulation files, one can determine the percentages of frequent and irregular users, along with the number of registered users compared to the general population. Typically, approximately one-third of a general population are registered as library users, indicating to the information professional the need to identify the needs of the two-thirds of the population who **do not** use the library, as well as refining knowledge of the information needs of the registered users. However, additional useful information must be attained from other sources described below.

Census Data

Census data are useful for making general statements about the ages of people within the boundaries of the library agency's service area. For example, a public library can determine the number of children who may be potential audience for a story hour designed for preschool-age children, or the number of retired people who may benefit from educational or recreational activities targeted for that age group. Segmenting the population by age groups enables the library professional staff to evaluate the potential audience for audience-directed programs and the known needs for that population group.

Generational books such as Gail Sheehy's *Passages* (1976) and *New Passages* (1995) provide guidelines for the changing concerns and issues that accompany the aging process. These guidelines enable library and information professionals to anticipate the information needs of segments of an agency's population and note its median age.

Census data also provide information concerning the number of households in a community, and the marital status, school enrollment, years of school completed, median education level, employment, occupations, industries, and commuting time and distance to work of individuals in the community. This information is helpful in constructing a profile of a community.

The most comprehensive and accurate information about residents of the United States is available through the U.S. Census Bureau at its web site: http://www.census.gov/index.html. This government agency provides current data based on the most recent decennial census, sometimes augmented with updated census information or estimates.

The U.S. Census Bureau web site provides easy access to *American Fact-Finder* (http://factfinder.census.gov/home/saff/main.html?_lang=en), a web page that enables the user to identify geographic areas by city, county, legislative district, and census tract. By using one or a combination of these areas, the user can obtain census data regarding the variables mentioned above, plus sex, disability, average annual income, national origins and languages, race and ethnicity, family relationships, veteran status, and housing.

One of the tools in *American FactFinder* is *State and County QuickFacts* (http://quickfacts.census.gov/qfd/). This web site enables the user to gather demographic data about his or her state and compare those data to national averages for such variables as general population, ethnic population, household income, travel time to work, and other economic indicators. County and city data are compared to state data by category. The comparative data are especially valuable for detecting unique or outstanding factors in a community and for providing quick, easy access to census facts about people, businesses, and geography. The home page provides a map of the United States; click on a state to access counties and cities. Data are available on individuals (e.g., ethnic groups, age, education), housing, businesses (e.g., non-farm employment, business ownership by ethnicity, sales volume), households (income, percent below the poverty level), and geography (land area, population per square mile).

Other useful information resources are available:

- *Statistical Abstract of the United States* (http://www.census.gov /compendia/statab/). This national data book provides statistics for the United States, with selected data for regions, divisions, states, metropolitan areas, cities, and foreign countries. Collected from reports and records of government and private agencies, the *Abstract* has been issued annually since 1878. A useful statistical fact book on the social, political, and economic aspects of the United States and includes many tables and charts. Available online and on CD-ROM.
- *State and Metropolitan Area Data Book* (http://www.census.gov /compendia/smadb/). This book features more than 1,500 data items for the United States as well as individual states, counties, and metropolitan areas from a variety of sources. The files include data published for 2005 population and housing unit estimates and many items from the 1990 and 2000 Census of Population and Housing. Topics included are age, agriculture, births, business establishments, communications, construction, cost of living, crime, deaths, education, elections, employment, energy, finance, government, health, households, housing, immigration, income, manufactures, marriages and divorces, media, natural resources, population, poverty, race and Hispanic origin, residence, retail sales, science and engineering, social services, tourism, transportation, and veterans. Data are from the U.S. Census Bureau and other federal statistical bureaus, governmental administrative and regulatory agencies, private research bodies, trade associations, insurance companies, health associations, educational associations, and philanthropic foundations.

- *Census Products Catalog* (http://www.census.gov/mp/www/cat/).
  Organized by subject categories; e.g., Census 2000, People, Housing,
  Foreign Trade, and Business Information, this catalog lists publications available through the Bureau of the Census Customer Services
  Center at 1-800-923-8282.
- *FedStats*, which has been available to the public since 1997, provides
  access to a full range of statistical information produced by the federal
  government from more than 100 federal agencies. The user can locate
  data and trend information on such topics as economic and population trends, crime, education, health care, aviation safety, energy
  use, farm production, and more. Data can be searched by state, city,
  county, or topic.

Using the Internet

The Internet is an excellent source of information about a municipality,
university, school system, public agency, or private sector organization.
The government data described above provide data for county and municipal bodies for comparison with state and national data on population,
economic, and political data. Similarly, the Internet is a source of data on
agencies at the local and state level, data that may not be available from
federal sources. State governments sponsor official portals for the states
and provide access to a great deal of governmental, cultural, educational,
economic, geographic, and recreational information that may be difficult
to find elsewhere.

Likewise, most municipalities have a web presence that also makes available a rich storehouse of information about that area. These web sites at the
state and local level are especially rich in the data useful in describing
lifestyles, as discussed later in this book. In addition, local chambers of commerce often maintain web sites that provide supplemental information
beyond that of the sites sponsored by government entities.

SUMMARY

This chapter focused on individuals as one of the four perspectives of a
community information needs analysis. As we consider the information
needs of individuals and design information services, we must consider the
elements of information psychology, how individuals become aware of an
information need, how they decide to act on that need (or not), how they
implement strategies in searching for information, how they display preferences for certain formats of media, assimilate the information using a
unique cognitive or learning style, and organize, store, retrieve, and use
information.

These principles are important to apply as data are gathered and services are planned for individuals. Sources of information about individuals in a community include government and other public sources, most of which are accessible via the Internet. Several federal web sites are described as fruitful sources of demographic information.

REFERENCES

American FactFinder. 2009. http://factfinder.census.gov/home/saff/main.html?_lang =en (accessed December 7, 2009).

Census Products Catalog. 2008. http://www.census.gov/mp/www/cat/ (accessed December 8, 2009).

FedStats. 2008. http://www.fedstats.gov/ (accessed December 8, 2009).

Greer, Roger C., Robert J. Grover, and Susan G. Fowler. 2007. *Introduction to the library and information professions.* Westport, CT and London: Libraries Unlimited.

Sheehy, Gail. 1976. *Passages: Predictable crises of adult life.* New York: Dutton.

———. 1995. *New passages: mapping your life across time.* New York: Random House.

State and County QuickFacts. http://quickfacts.census.gov/qfd/ (accessed December 8, 2009).

State and Metropolitan Area Data Book. 2009. http://www.census.gov/compendia/ smadb/ (accessed December 8, 2009).

The 2010 Statistical Abstract: The National Data Book. 2010. http://www .census.gov/compendia/statab (accessed February 28, 2010).

United States Census Bureau. http://www.census.gov/index.html (accessed December 7, 2009).

CHAPTER 7

Studying the Information Needs of Groups

CHAPTER OVERVIEW

A community in any environment—whether a municipality, private enterprise, university, government agency, or school—is complex. In this chapter we examine various groups in order to determine their information needs. The term "groups" is defined with examples, and sources of community information about groups are explored and discussed. We also suggest what to look for—implications about groups for translation into information services.

IDENTIFYING GROUPS IN A COMMUNITY

The information professional conducting an information needs assessment must identify the various groups in the community, their characteristics and information needs. The definition of groups in Chapter 4 is "a formal or informal organization which meets and functions regularly." Groups are formed around common interests, and the exploration of groups provides a sketch of individuals' interests in the community. As emphasized in Greer and Hale (1982, 362), groups are an indication of the service area's sense of community:

Is the focus on community life in the neighborhood? Do people get together in organizations within the service area, or is their orientation toward a larger perhaps metropolitan community? This gives a clue as to whether there is a sense of community among the residents that the library can build on, or whether it is a community only in the geographic sense—people living in proximity. Libraries serving these two different types of communities must approach their tasks in radically different ways.

Unlike an agency, a group typically does not have an office or telephone for contact. Examples of groups in a community would be service organizations (Lions Clubs, Rotary, etc.), service fraternities and sororities, and clubs dedicated to an interest or hobby. In smaller communities, the local newspaper usually includes club news and their meeting schedules. In larger communities, neighborhood or suburban newspapers often perform the same function.

To systematically identify and analyze groups, it is helpful to categorize them. For example, a matrix might be constructed using these categories:

- Recreational
- Social
- Religious
- Cultural
- School
- Hobbies
- Ethnic
- Age-related
- Environmental
- Political
- Project-oriented
- Commercial
- Vocational/occupational

In a school community, groups would include school student organizations, e.g., marching band, debate club, science club, photography club, library club, and other organizations that cater to student interests. Other groups might be faculty-teaching teams, and in a larger school system, school principals may meet as a group. Likewise, department chairs, the parent-teacher association, and the school board are examples of other groups.

Academic communities, like schools, have clubs segregated by interest group, e.g., Math Club, Psychology Club, and Fellowship of Christian Athletes. Other groups would include administrative groups, e.g., Deans' Council, advisory groups to schools and colleges, fraternities and sororities, alumni groups, and various committees on campus. Special library communities will also have formal and informal groups and committees within the staff for organizational, administrative, educational, and recreational purposes.

Groups may have information needs that can be addressed successfully by an information professional; however, the informality of the group can hinder attempts to learn of the group's purpose and information needs. The groups themselves may be elusive; since they may not have phone numbers, it may be difficult to identify the leaders in order to engage in a conversation about interests and information needs. Suggestions for systematically identifying and contacting groups are the next topic for discussion.

Sources of Information

Because groups are informal, identifying groups in a community can be more challenging than identifying agencies, which are usually listed in a phone directory. As noted above, newspapers within the community or agency are good sources for identifying groups, clubs, and various organizations. Directories may be available in print or on web pages. The groups may have newsletters, perhaps in electronic format. Many groups have a web site, and this source can be effective in making contact, and study of the web site can help determine the group's possible information needs. Another good source, and perhaps the best, is people. Talk with community residents to determine which are the most popular clubs and other organizations. From these random conversations will come a general understanding of the names and relative popularity and activity of groups within the community. Still another fruitful source is bulletin boards scattered throughout the community. Make it a point to walk around and to study bulletin boards; take notes of groups and their activities, along with contact information.

It is important at this point in the community analysis to collect impressions, not detailed data. We recommend avoiding the creation of a group or club database as part of the community analysis. While the community analysis report may include a recommendation to create a club directory, such a project will substantially extend the time required to complete the community analysis.

The best place to begin gathering data about groups in a municipality is the local newspaper (either online or in print). Carefully read every item in the newspaper on a daily basis for a week, perhaps twice if it is a weekly publication. Include in your analysis the news items, obituaries (noting any local organizations mentioned), classified ads, and editorials. Every item is a potential source of information. We suggest creating a matrix like that in Figure 7.1 to record the trends that you are observing.

Since you are looking for trends, you may make a hash mark (#) in the appropriate box, or you may wish to list groups by name, to be sure they are counted only once, and for future reference. Keep in mind the following point made by Greer and Hale (1982, 363):

> You are looking for patterns, attempting to become aware of interests. Often librarians are aware of where the interests lie, but until they begin a community analysis they are not sure of themselves. They have

Figure 7.1   Group Matrix.

Purpose	Informal Groups	Clubs	Service Organizations
Recreation			
Education			
Religious			
Political			
Religious			
Cultural			
School			
Hobbies			
Ethnic			
Age-related			
Environmental			
Political			
Project-oriented			
Commercial			
Vocational/ occupational			

not allowed themselves to take the time to ask, "So what for the library?" and to use these data for planning systematically.

What are some groups that we may find in various kinds of libraries or information agencies? Examples of these groups are found below.

Examples of Groups

The types of groups, of course, will vary with the type of organization that we work in. In addition, the size of organization will make a huge difference; larger municipalities, colleges, schools, and corporations will offer a larger range of groups than smaller organizations. Below we use the categories outlined above and suggest examples of groups by four types of organizations: municipalities and public libraries, schools, colleges and universities, and private enterprises and government agencies.

Municipalities

As noted above, local newspapers are a good source of information when conducting a community analysis for a public library. Talking with library staff and clients is a good way of discovering active groups in a community. Directories can be helpful, and some groups may be listed in the yellow pages of a phone directory (most will not). A walk-around or drive-around in a community can be fruitful as well. Below are examples of types of groups that may be active in a town or city.

- Recreational: athletic teams and clubs, chess club, dance club, sports leagues (bowling, baseball, softball, basketball, track, football, etc.), bicycling clubs, motorcycle clubs, arts & crafts groups, YMCA groups, skating rinks, swimming pools
- Social: gourmet cooking clubs, support groups (e.g., Alcoholics Anonymous, Narcotics Anonymous), Parents Without Partners, singles clubs
- Religious: churches and synagogues, religious women's groups and men's groups, religious committees or ministries, governing councils, ministerial alliances, inter-faith groups, Bible study groups, worship groups
- Cultural: bands and orchestras, choral groups, book discussion groups, genealogy societies, historical societies, study and forum groups, art societies, dramatic groups, literary societies
- School: parent-teacher association, alumni (see also *schools* below), better school groups, adult education groups, teacher organizations
- Hobbies: camera/photography clubs, stamp collectors, quilting circles, athletic team supporters, collectors' groups
- Ethnic: Hispanic, African-American, American Indian, Chinese, etc.
- Age-related: retired teachers and other professionals
- Environmental: Sierra Club, Audubon Society
- Political: local political parties, Young Republicans, Young Democrats, Mothers Against Drunk Drivers (MADD), good government leagues, patriotic and veterans' associations, taxpayer associations, community planning associations, community councils, environmental groups
- Project-oriented: service clubs (e.g., Kiwanis, Lions Club, Optimist Club, Rotary Club, Sertoma Club), cooperatives, industrial development organizations
- Commercial: dentists, physicians, business owners, investors, real estate associations
- Vocational/occupational: unions, guilds, retail merchants' associations, farmers' associations, boards of banks and corporations, professional associations

Schools

Here again, the school newspaper can be a good source for identifying groups within a school, especially those that are most active. Walking the halls and noting material on bulletin boards will also reveal activities sponsored by groups. Talking with the principal, counselors, and random students will be helpful. The school web page will also list various groups sponsored by the school. Below are examples of groups by category.

- Recreational: interscholastic sports teams, intramural teams, cheerleaders, fan groups, conditioning clubs
- Social: school spirit club
- Religious: groups organized by denomination, Bible study groups, prayer groups, interfaith groups
- Cultural: arts clubs, chorale, musical groups, dance team, orchestra, marching band, theatre productions, thespians, science fiction and fantasy
- Hobbies: photography
- Ethnic: Black Student Association, Asian Student Association, etc.
- Environmental: backpacking club
- Political: Gay/Straight Alliance (and other gay/lesbian groups), Students Against Destructive Decisions (SADD), student council, freshman/sophomore/junior/senior class councils, athletic council
- Project-oriented: student clubs affiliated with community service organizations (e.g., Key Club/Kiwanis, Leo Club/Lions)
- Commercial: Future Business Leaders of America
- Vocational/occupational: clubs by course of study (e.g., astronomy, biology, chemistry, business, languages, psychology, science, technology studies), debate/forensics, Future Educators of America, school newspaper, yearbook, school television station
- Other: National Honor Society

Colleges and Universities

All of the methods for identifying groups in schools will apply here: perusing the college or university newspaper, walking around the campus and noting material on bulletin boards, and talking with students and faculty will be helpful. Visiting with a leader in the student affairs office will be very helpful, and the college web site will list various groups. Below are examples of groups by category.

- Recreational: interscholastic sports teams, intramural teams, cheerleaders, fan groups, conditioning clubs, sports clubs (e.g., soccer, fencing, karate)

- Social: fraternities, sororities, faculty and staff social groups
- Religious: student groups organized by denomination, interfaith groups
- Cultural: arts clubs, chorale, instrumental groups, dance team, debate team, film study groups, French Club, German Club (and other language organizations), orchestra, marching band, theatre productions, thespians, book discussion groups
- Hobbies: photography, stamp collecting
- Ethnic: such groups as the Arabic Student Association, Asian Student Association, Black Student Union, Chinese Student Association, Hispanic American Student Association, International Student Association, Muslim Student Association, Thai Student Association, Taiwanese Student Association, etc.
- Environmental: backpacking club, biology club
- Political: Gay/Straight Alliance (and other gay/lesbian groups), Students Against Destructive Decisions (SADD), student government, freshman/sophomore/junior/senior class councils, athletic council, honors program council, residence hall governance
- Project-oriented: school newspaper, yearbook, television or radio station
- Vocational/occupational: clubs by majors of study (e.g., accounting, astronomy, biology, chemistry, computer science, computer information systems, business, engineers, languages, marketing, MBA club, physics, psychology, public affairs, rehabilitation programs, science, sociology, technology studies), debate/forensics, Future Educators of America, Student Chapter of the American Library Association, Association for Computing Machinery, honor societies by discipline, e.g., Alpha Kappa Delta (sociology), Delta Pi Epsilon (business graduates), Phi Beta Lambda (business students), Pi Gamma Mu (social science), Sigma Tau Delta (English)
- Other: faculty groups (part-time or temporary, non-tenured, associate professors, professors, retired), honors program, nontraditional student association

Private Enterprise and Government Agencies

Companies and government agencies can be studied in much the same way as schools—the company or agency newsletter can be a good source for identifying groups. Walking the halls and reading information on bulletin boards will also reveal active groups. Talking with company or agency managers and random employees will be very helpful. The company web site, usually aimed at consumers, may not be the most fruitful source for groups. Below are examples of groups by category.

- Recreational: sports groups and company teams
- Social: informal groups to socialize
- Religious: study or prayer groups by denomination or religion
- Cultural: music, cooking, language study, arts, travel groups
- School: university alumni groups, classes offered by the company
- Hobbies: various leisure activities, e.g., gardening, collecting, photography
- Ethnic: groups by ethnicity or country of origin
- Age-related: young marrieds, singles, retirees
- Environmental: Sierra Club, hiking club
- Political: groups with causes both inside and outside the company
- Project-oriented: task forces, committees within the company
- Commercial: investment clubs
- Vocational/occupational: groups with similar jobs

WHAT YOU WANT TO KNOW

As information is gathered about groups, additional information is needed in order to identify the information needs of groups. The following are questions to ask during the data-gathering process:

1. Have I identified the names and number of organizations and groups?
2. Can I obtain estimates of the active membership of each organization or group?
3. How do I determine which groups get things done, which are prestigious?
4. What are implications for time required for the group's activities?
5. What times of day, or what days and seasons, are significant to these groups and activities?
6. Is the community morning- or evening-oriented?

These questions can be answered through newspaper scanning, web site analysis, and focus groups comprised of selected community members active in organizations—the "movers and shakers" in the community.

IMPLICATIONS FOR LIBRARY AND INFORMATION SERVICES

Groups are a measure of interests in a community. When these interests are identified, how does the library's collection include resources on these topics? Perhaps the library could co-sponsor programs with groups on their topics of interest. By systematically observing the activities of local groups, library planners can tune in to the interests of people in the community.

Figure 7.2   Summary of Group Information.

Organization Name	Approximate membership	Notable activities	Significant times, days, seasons	Implications for Service	Possible collaboration
Group 1					
Group 2					
Group 3					
Group 4					
Group 5					

Furthermore, data from such a study can lead to a discussion with group leaders about library services and what groups can do to support the library. A library or information agency must be an integral part of its community to be transformative, and awareness of interests can lead to win-win collaboration between groups and the library.

The chart in Figure 7.2 can be used to summarize data gleaned from the community analysis.

SUMMARY

In this chapter, we identified various groups and suggested the means for determining their information needs. A description of a community's groups is a profile of the interests in a community, interests that should guide the planning of library and information services. Sources of community information about groups were explored and discussed. We also suggested information sources in order to plan services and possible collaboration with groups.

REFERENCE

Greer, Roger C., and Martha L. Hale. 1982. "The community analysis process." In *Public librarianship: a reader*, ed. J. Robbins-Carter, 358–366. Littleton, CO: Libraries Unlimited.

CHAPTER 8

Studying the Information Needs of Agencies

CHAPTER OVERVIEW

In this chapter we define the term "agencies," give examples of agencies, and their role in the community is discussed. Methods for gathering information about agencies are explored. Characteristics of agencies in a variety of environments are investigated, with implications for information services.

DEFINITION OF AGENCIES

As discussed in Chapter 4, groups are usually informal organizations, but **agencies** are formal parts of a larger organization, and these agencies provide a service or a product. We can assume that agencies exist because they fulfill the needs for their services or products within the community. Agencies are identified and studied for reasons similar to the study of groups. Greer and Hale (1982, 363) identify the following reasons for studying agencies:

1. Agencies supply additional information to amplify the library staff's understanding of the community and attempt to limit the bias that would come from only one vantage point.
2. They collect data on what else is available for community residents that can complement services offered by the library.
3. They use the data to choose from among alternative patterns of service.

For example, a community will have such agencies as police and fire departments, public libraries, a human resources department, recreation department, schools, and numerous other agencies that have a mission within the municipality. Among other types of communities or organizations, schools, colleges or universities, and private or public agencies themselves have internal agencies as well. A community analysis requires assessing information needs by identifying and analyzing the missions and characteristics of agencies serving the community.

Other agencies that are very important to a municipality are the businesses established within the community. As with public agencies, each private enterprise in a community has a mission that it must fulfill to stay in business. Some enterprises may be large enough to staff their own library or information services, but many are small enough that they cannot afford an in-house information staff; consequently, the public library may be the best source for addressing small business information needs.

Our experience with public libraries indicates that 25–35 percent of the population is reached by library services. While we do not have data for other types of information agencies, it is safe to say that a larger service population percentage is desirable, and information professionals are continuously challenged to reach the non-users. One way of increasing the service population is to provide information services through agencies in the community. Helping agency personnel do their jobs better is providing library and information service indirectly to individuals in a community. Working with agencies can serve the general public (or the school/academic/special clientele) indirectly by serving the agency, which in turn may serve the public better because the agency gets the information needed to provide better service or products.

The first step in developing a relationship with agencies is to discover which agencies exist within the service area of the library or information agency.

Sources of Information

The first challenge is identification of agencies in your community. Since they are formal organizations, a telephone directory is a good source to check first. The sources of information for agencies are similar to that of groups. Walk-arounds (or drive-arounds), newspapers, especially the yellow pages, directories, and people in the community are all good sources of information regarding the dominant and most active agencies in the community. Because the Internet is now a ubiquitous source of information, a "virtual tour" of a community can be very informative. However, we advise the reader to take a systematic approach to discovering agencies by following a procedure similar to that of identifying groups:

1. Create categories
2. Collect rough estimates of the number of agencies in each category
3. Refine those estimates when you need more information to choose between services that can be offered

It is helpful to remember that categories are general suggestions for identifying differing kinds of agencies and services/products. Use the list below as a draft list, and revise the categories to suit your community and your information agency's needs.

Identifying Agencies

A good way to start making a list of categories is to use the list below, or to consult a telephone directory for your municipality, school, college or university, or private enterprise. In general, agencies may be categorized as follows to create a checklist for a community analysis:

- Government
- Religious
- Health Care
- Cultural
- Educational
- Business
- Informational: With whom can the library cooperate?

The above list is not exhaustive, and readers may wish to add to it for their own communities. Examples are provided below for municipalities, schools, higher education, and private enterprises and public agencies.

Examples of Agencies

Municipalities

Municipalities are possibly the most complex communities for which to identify agencies. If the public library district is suburban, library clientele will attain many services in the urban center; however, for practical considerations, the suburban public library should restrict its study of agencies to its service area as much as possible, recognizing that some services in nearby suburbs may also provide needed and frequently used services to residents in your service area.

The best sources of information for agencies in municipalities are telephone yellow pages for the metropolitan area or suburb. Web pages for the community often list local service agencies for the convenience of residents and new arrivals to the community. The chamber of commerce is a good source for lists of services provided by agencies; a visit to the chamber offices or to the chamber's web site should be an early visit by the community analysis data-gathering team. It should be noted that chambers of commerce often do a better, more comprehensive job of listing cultural events and promoting the activities of the city than do the official web sites maintained by the city; the latter often focus on government agencies, while the chamber of commerce is more focused on promoting the city to its residents, visitors, and private enterprises.

Below are examples of agency types that may be helpful as you identify agencies in your municipality.

Government   Frequently found federal agencies include such offices as military services, the Corps of Engineers, the Department of Agriculture, Department of Interior (administration of wildlife refuges), Social Security Administration, Internal Revenue Service, Post Office, offices of elected representatives and senators, and the Department of Veterans Affairs.

State governmental agencies may include a National Guard recruiting office, department of human services, department of revenue, driver's license bureau or registry of motor vehicles, department of transportation, highway maintenance department, insurance department, social services, and department of wildlife and parks.

County government agencies might include ambulance services, animal control services and shelter, appraiser, county attorney, conservation district, council on aging, county clerk, county commission, county counselor-at-law, personnel office, treasurer, court services, district court, engineer, extension office, fire district, health department, library district, motor vehicle department, museum, noxious weed department, recreation center, road and bridge department, sheriff, recycling center, and water district.

Local government agencies might include an airport, ambulance and fire department, animal control shelter, arts council, municipal golf course, health department or hospital, inspections/codes/permits and engineers, transportation service, fire and ambulance service, library, museum, parks and zoos, police, recreation center, refuse department, recycling center, household hazards and waste center, sewage department, street department, water treatment plant, city council or legislative body and elected officials, and social or human services department.

Religious   Both predominant and minority religious service groups in a community are listed in telephone directory yellow pages, usually by denomination. Entries may include times for worship services, children's services, and youth group meetings. Such services as nursery, Bible study groups, and youth programs may be listed. The availability of a circulating library collection may be noted. Support agencies might include church-related counseling services, bookstores, nursery or preschools, thrift shops, and meeting rooms.

Health Care   Health care agencies include those facilities that provide a wide range of medical care. The U.S. Department of Labor Bureau of Labor

Statistics (http://www.bls.gov/oco/cg/cgs035.htm) lists the following nine segments of the health care industry:

- **Hospitals.** Hospitals provide complete medical care, ranging from diagnostic services, to surgery, to continuous nursing care. Some hospitals specialize in the treatment of the mentally ill, or cancer patients, or children. Hospital-based care may be on an inpatient (overnight) or outpatient basis.
- **Nursing and residential care facilities.** Nursing care facilities provide inpatient nursing, rehabilitation, and health-related personal care to those who need continuous nursing care, but do not require hospital services.
- **Physicians' offices.** About 37 percent of all health care establishments fall into this industry segment.
- **Dentists' offices.** About one out of every five health care establishments is a dentist's office.
- **Home health care services.** Skilled nursing or medical care is sometimes provided in the home, under a physician's supervision. Home health care services are provided mainly to the elderly. The development of in-home medical technologies, substantial cost savings, and patients' preference for care in the home have helped change this once-small segment of the industry into one of the fastest growing parts of the economy.
- **Offices of other health practitioners.** This segment of the health care industry includes the offices of chiropractors, optometrists, podiatrists, occupational and physical therapists, psychologists, audiologists, speech-language pathologists, dietitians, and other health care practitioners.
- **Outpatient care centers.** The diverse establishments in this group include kidney dialysis centers, outpatient mental health and substance abuse centers, health maintenance organization medical centers, and freestanding ambulatory surgical and emergency centers.
- **Other ambulatory health care services.** This relatively small industry segment includes ambulance and helicopter transport services, blood and organ banks, and other ambulatory health care services, such as pacemaker monitoring services and smoking cessation programs.
- **Medical and diagnostic laboratories.** Medical and diagnostic laboratories provide analytic or diagnostic services to the medical profession or directly to patients following a physician's prescription.

Many of these health care agencies may be found in any municipality.

Cultural   Cultural agencies abound in a municipality, and many are embedded in local and state agencies. For example, schools and colleges promote cultural events through their art, literature, music, dance, and theatre departments.

In addition, a local government may sponsor an arts council that stages and promotes concerts and hosts touring theatre and music companies. Other cultural agencies sponsored by government include concert halls, museums (especially local history), libraries (school, public, special, and college/university), art galleries, and zoos.

Among commercial cultural agencies are movie theaters, art galleries, and commercial museums (e.g., wax museums).

Educational   Educational agencies include public and private schools for various age groups: preschool, elementary, middle school, high school, community college, four-year college, and universities. Among post-high school educational institutions are a growing number of vocational schools which prepare people for a variety of specialized occupations such as truck driving, computer technician, cosmetology, landscape management, computer programming and software engineering, game design and development, network security, web design and e-commerce, drafting and design, plumbing, welding, dental assistant, medical assistant, air conditioning and refrigeration repair, construction, food service, teacher's assistant, aircraft pilot training, and automotive maintenance.

Data collection on educational agencies and institutions should note whether their educational programs are supported by a library and/or Internet information services. Also, it should be noted if these programs have classroom facilities, or conduct their programs electronically.

Businesses   Businesses are usually the most prolific agencies in a community. While the yellow pages of a phone directory, online business directory, or local chamber of commerce web site may provide the most comprehensive listing of businesses, the number and variety of businesses can be overwhelming in larger municipalities. A drive-around can be productive to get a sense of the themes or dominant businesses that emerge. For example, in a community in the American Midwest, agricultural businesses may stand out—implement sales, tractor sales, farm equipment repair and parts, farm and ranch suppliers, feed stores, fencing, fertilizer sales, and farm real estate brokers.

Another possible way to narrow the list of businesses in a community is to pay attention to and list those listed more than 20 times (or another number of your choosing) in a phone directory or list of businesses provided by the local chamber of commerce.

All business organizations have a need for management-oriented information, which is common to all organizations offering products or services. Management and accounting skills are required by the managers of even the smallest of organizations. A library can make a significant difference by collecting resources addressing these common needs.

Schools

Agencies in a school district or school building are those offices that serve the students and faculty in a specialized way. For example, the school nurse, psychologist, library, athletic department, and music department are examples of agencies within a school that serve a mission for the school. School agencies can be identified most easily by consulting a printed directory or the school web page. A walk-around is also recommended.

Below is a listing of agencies typically found in a school district.

- Academic departments
- Athletics (interscholastic)
- Attendance office
- Board of Education
- Bookstore
- Buildings & grounds
- Business office
- Counselors
- Food services
- Health services
- Human resources
- Information technology
- Laboratories: science, computers
- Library services
- Registrar
- Security office
- Student support services
- Transportation

The data collection process should include an attempt to determine whether these agencies receive or need any information to support their services.

Colleges and Universities

Academic agencies also include the offices of departments, schools, and colleges within a university. Agencies include those offices that serve the students, staff, and faculty of the institution. Examples of these agencies are listed below. A campus directory should be consulted for specific names, either a printed copy or online at the campus web site.

- Academic departments
- Administrative offices
- Alumni relations
- Athletics (intercollegiate)
- Bookstore
- Buildings and grounds
- Business services
- Career services
- Counseling center
- Disability services
- Faculty governance office
- Financial aid office
- Food services
- Graduate studies
- Health center
- Human resources
- Laboratories
- Libraries
- Lifelong learning/ continuing education
- Mail center
- Marketing
- Multicultural programs & services

- Parking services
- Police & safety
- Printing services
- Public affairs office
- Registration
- Research and grants
- Residence halls
- Student affairs office
- Student government
- Student publications (newspaper, yearbook, etc.)
- Technology and computing services
- University advancement
- University archives

Private Enterprise and Government Agencies

Agencies in the private sector or in government are those offices within an organization that provide services to the organization. Some of the same examples from colleges and universities would be relevant, such as human resources, printing, budget office, etc.

Employees of companies or government agencies, as well as customers and clients, may derive important services from agencies outside the company or government agency. For example, the public library may be consulted for information resources, or government offices may be frequent sources of information. Observation and consultation with key personnel can be useful in identifying the external agencies that play vital roles as sources of information.

We urge you to review the examples of agencies listed under the heading "Colleges and Universities" above to see possible categories of agencies that may exist in your company or in the nearby community.

IMPLICATIONS FOR LIBRARY AND INFORMATION SERVICES

Because agencies provide a service, they are often information intensive. Current and accurate information is needed by agencies to serve the organization effectively. Information professionals can provide that information, if the information needs of agencies are effectively identified. In a sense, the public library could serve as a special library for certain agencies in their community. Likewise, school and academic libraries could provide information services to internal or external agencies that would benefit both the library and the agency. Customized information services available to businesses could provide an opportunity for entrepreneurship, an opportunity to derive income from services charged to participating agencies.

On a very practical level, libraries serve individuals who work in agencies, and the public, special, or academic library can serve working individuals with information that they can use in their work. With this in mind, librarians can knowingly order books and other information resources that address the needs of the people working in these agencies. On a more creative and entrepreneurial level, an information service can be provided to staff members in agencies to improve services in those agencies. Yet another opportunity for collaboration is for the library to disseminate information for the agencies in the vicinity. For example, the public and academic library can provide brochures and such items as tax forms for various government agencies.

In any case, it is important for librarians and other information professionals to know and understand the agencies in their service area in order to provide the services needed by those agencies and the individuals who work in them. Striving for partnerships with agencies is a recommended goal in order for libraries to offer vital, needed services and resources within a community.

SUMMARY

In this chapter, the term "agencies" is defined as formal parts of a larger organization, and agencies' roles in the community are discussed. Methods for gathering information about agencies are explored, and examples of agencies in municipalities, schools, colleges and universities, the private sector, and government agencies are discussed. In order to provide information services that meet the needs of clientele, library and information professionals must be knowledgeable of the agencies within a library's service area so that services may be customized to meet those needs. Libraries and agencies can collaborate to further their missions and benefit their constituencies.

REFERENCES

Greer, Roger C., and Martha L. Hale. 1982. The community analysis process. In *Public librarianship: a reader*, ed. J. Robbins-Carter, 358–366. Littleton, CO: Libraries Unlimited.

Healthcare. U.S. Department of Labor Bureau of Labor Statistics, *Career guide to industries*. http://www.bls.gov/oco/cg/cgs035.htm (accessed December 8, 2009).

CHAPTER 9

Lifestyles

CHAPTER OVERVIEW

"Lifestyles" is defined, and elements of lifestyle are identified and described. Sources of information for determining the culture of a community are explored, along with implications for library and information services.

DEFINITION OF LIFESTYLES

The fourth category of our community analysis model is lifestyles. This term refers to the unique culture of the community: its history, values, customs, traditions, topography, climate, leisure activities, and other attributes that make a community unique. These characteristics have an enormous impact on the types of information resources and services required by members of a community.

First, we will identify and define these characteristics and their relevance to community information needs.

- History: What does the history of the community tell us about the community as it is today?
- Values: What are the primary concerns and values of the community residents? What are the most important elements in the lives of the residents?
- Customs: What traditions or rituals are a regular part of the residents' lives?
- Topography: What topographical features are prominent in the community? How do these features influence traffic and everyday living?

- Climate: How does the climate influence activities and life in the community?
- Leisure activities: How do people spend their leisure time? Which activities are most common?
- Transportation: How do people move from one place to another? Is the library or information service easily accessible to all potential clients?
- Communication: Is the communication infrastructure supportive of easy and frequent communication among the community residents? Are there blockages to effective communication?
- "Community-ness": Is there a sense of community? Do the community members see themselves as part of this community? To what extent is there community pride?
- Economic life: How would you characterize the economic level of residents? Is the community affluent, or is it "hanging on" economically? How does the economic condition affect lifestyle?
- Social issues: What are the dominant social concerns of the community members? What issues appear to hold their attention at the present time? How many churches or religious centers exist in the community? Is there a dominant religion?

These elements of a community's lifestyle apply to communities regardless of type, whether a municipality, school, college or university, public agency, or private enterprise. We will explore each of these elements, and while we will not use specific examples or explore differences by type of community, the reader will be able to apply these principles to any type of community. In our discussion, we are focusing on the public library community; extrapolating to other communities can be done, but we leave that to you, the reader.

The components of lifestyle can influence the types of information services offered in a community of any type: municipality, academic environment, school library, or special library clientele. What are the implications in your community for each of the factors?

EXPLORING CULTURE IN A COMMUNITY

The four perspectives of a community analysis (individuals, groups, agencies, and lifestyle) will enable the staff members to identify the unique qualities of a community and to identify agencies and groups who are leading contributors to the lifestyle of the community. It is a systematic approach for collecting data for making decisions about information services to be offered. Lifestyle includes a wide range of characteristics contributing to any community's heritage and uniqueness. In order to study lifestyle, this topic is divided into components with suggested sources for each.

History

Elements of a Community's History

History is a relevant causative factor in the evolution of a community's culture. To understand the characteristics of a community in its present state, with its current population, community-ness, corporate agencies providing services and products, and current economic prospects, it is necessary to explore the historical evolution of the community in all of these areas. Studying a community without paying attention to its history is comparable to buying a house without an inspection and without reference to community services, location, and all of the characteristics that go with that.

A community's history can be explored by addressing the following questions:

- What are the origins of this community, and why was it established where it is? How has it evolved to what it is today, who are the key people in its evolution, and what are key historical events?
- What has been the influence of historical events and conditions on today's lifestyles in the community?
- Where did the early leaders of the community come from during its development, and which of their contributions are still evident?
- When were infrastructure elements such as water, sewers, paved roads, etc. developed? What is their current state of repair? If the infrastructure is in bad shape, it dominates a community's attention.
- What are the chief conditions, circumstances, resources, or factors of location which determined this community's development to its current state?
- What were the important steps in the economic development of the area?
- What movements have swept through this community at one time or another? What impact have these movements had?
- What were the important economic events or circumstances that contributed to both expansion and contraction of the community? What kinds of manufacturing, marketing, or financial activities were started and when?
- What historical archives exist and where are they? Who is making an effort to maintain and expand them? Is there a role for the library to provide leadership in this area?
- What elements of the community's history are people proud of?

Sources of Historical Information

These historical questions can be explored through reading histories, reports, newspapers, and documents of the community and can be found in libraries, local museums, archives, and public records. Talking with longtime residents of the community can be very informative in answering some these questions.

The history of a group or agency can also be located through records kept by the organization. Another source of the history is the oral history of long-time members who may have been founders of the organization. Sometimes these accounts lack accuracy but can be a good starting point for historical background. The objective of this effort is to discover areas of interest in the community and how the library can contribute.

Values

Elements of a Community's Values

Values, or mores, have a profound influence on the dynamics of community activity as well as the way in which the community evolved. Evidence of values can be addressed by answering these questions:

- How are children perceived in the community? How are senior citizens perceived?
- Is the community diverse in ethnicity, religions, and cultures? Is this diversity embraced?
- What kinds of non-profits or charitable organizations exist and thrive?
- Are there services for the indigent?
- What is the ratio of religious centers to bars in the community? Do most of the people attend religious services, or do they merely pay lip service to religion?
- What are the primary concerns and values of the community residents?
- What are the most important elements in the lives of the residents?
- Is the recreational culture well organized with well-groomed sports facilities, or is it a "street ball" community?
- Is the local newspaper independent, conservative, or liberal? Are there multiple local newspapers with different political views?
- Are people pragmatic—do they want to get things done quickly, or would they rather discuss the philosophy or morality of an issue before acting?
- What are the apparent moral values of the community? The library must be aware of these values.

Sources of Information about Values

These questions can best be answered by talking with long-time members of the community, especially community leaders. As the history is gleaned through interviews, so can the values be explored. Another good source of values statements are found in the mission statements of organizations along with annual reports, minutes of governance board meetings, and other official documents of the organization.

Customs

Elements of a Community's Customs

What traditions, rituals, or annual events are a regular part of the residents' lives? Traditions are developed as part of a community's history. These traditions may be recorded as part of a history, but they may be passed on as part of the oral tradition. Such traditions might include an annual Christmas, Memorial Day, or Fourth of July parade. Communities often have annual festivals to promote economic activity and celebrate their history; for example, the summer "Bean Hole Day" in Pequot Lakes, Minnesota when they dig a hole with a back hoe, light a fire in it, and build up a base of embers and lower a covered bean pot into it with a cherry picker to cook for three days. It is then pulled up, uncovered, and a community festival begins.

In many Midwestern communities there are rodeos, such as the annual rodeo in Cheyenne, Wyoming, or the Tulip Festival in Holland, Michigan. Many communities of various sizes have developed such traditions. Chicago has a "Taste of Chicago" festival that promotes foods from the city's ethnic sub-communities.

What kinds of personal celebrations are customary in your particular community? How do residents celebrate and commemorate births, first communions, marriages, anniversaries, deaths? The celebration of historical events is one example of community-wide traditions that may be recorded. Costumes, dances, dress codes, and expected behaviors may not be recorded but are part of the expectations for all members of the organization.

Sources of Information about Customs

A community's traditions can best be determined through interviews of long-time community or organization residents. You may also search in local newspapers for articles documenting community events.

Topographical Features

Elements of Topographical Features

Just as prominent topographical characteristics influence the origin and development of a community and remain a very strong component of a community analysis study, topographic features such as rivers, creeks, and mountains impact how the community develops and how people move around the community. Included in these features is the existence of highways, rivers, and buildings that may influence the lifestyle. Physical and geographical features can influence the lifestyle of any community.

While assessing which topographic features to explore, remember to focus on those features that have an impact on the library; we are not assessing property values. The following questions can guide exploration of this topic:

- What geographic characteristics suggest certain lifestyles and influence patterns of behavior?
- What issues are provoked by the existence of topographical features, e.g., the need for modern bridges?
- Where are the identifiable neighborhoods or clustering of community residents? How do topographical characteristics influence the development of neighborhoods?
- What issues are provoked by the existence of topographical features?

Sources of Information about Topographical Features

Geographical features can be identified by personal observation during a drive-around or through a study of maps and analysis of planning agency documents. Focus groups and individual interviews can be good sources of information on how topography influences lifestyles because much of this information is not published.

Climate

Elements of a Community's Climate

Climate is a basic determinant of lifestyle characteristics. Heat, humidity, and cold can influence a community's activities and customs. Climate has a profound impact on a community, from the design of enclosed malls or open malls, to the design of public and private buildings. For example, in areas with warm climates such as Florida and Hawaii, architects may design some buildings with open hallways on the building's exterior.

A community's climate can be identified by addressing the following questions:

- How does the climate influence activities and life in the community?
- To what extent has climate controlled the evolution of the community, and to what extent has its impact been reduced by community infrastructure? For example, shopping malls in Minneapolis are

enclosed, while shopping malls in southern California and Florida may be done in an open-air style. Minneapolis, Indianapolis, and other northern cities have enclosed walkways in downtown areas.

Sources of Information about Climate

Climate information can be identified by personal observation, the study of climate maps, and composite weather data available from the National Weather Service. Conversations with longtime residents will also offer a perspective.

Leisure Activities

Identifying Leisure Activities

Leisure or recreational activities are those pastimes in which people engage in their spare time for enjoyment. This includes both dynamic activities involving individual participation (e.g., bowling, softball leagues, badminton, golf, tennis, skiing, snowboarding, hunting, fishing, and knitting) and passive or spectator participation (such as watching major league baseball, professional football, professional golf, basketball, and other spectator sports). Public and commercial recreational facilities and programs can be thought of as supplements to the spontaneous employment of leisure time by individuals and intimate family and friendship groups.

The following questions address leisure activities in a community:

- How do people spend their leisure time? Which activities are most common?
- How do topography and climate influence the development and enjoyment of leisure activities such as skiing, camping, sailing, outdoor sports, or swimming?
- How much infrastructure is required for a leisure activity to be enjoyed? For which age groups?
- What are the locations, conditions, seasons, days, and hours of significance?
- What proportions of the population area are interested in specific activities?
- Are interests and patterns of recreation constant or changing?
- What are the local sports interests?
- How many area parks are there and where are they located? What is their accessibility?
- Are leisure activities organized for groups or are they individual in nature?
- What will people pay for? How much do they pay per year?

- To what extent are the tax-supported programs and facilities used by the public?
- Are the available facilities related to specific age groups?
- Is there an organization, widely representative of volunteer citizens and municipal officials, whose principal function is continuously planning for recreation in the community?

Sources of Information about Leisure Activities

Information about the leisure activities of a community can be found by visiting local park and recreation agencies, interviewing agency staff, reviewing telephone directories, visiting sports stores, reading the sports pages of local newspapers, listening to local TV and radio stations, visiting hobby shops, and visiting the leisure or recreation pages of local government and chamber of commerce web sites. Go into a sporting goods store and determine how much space is devoted to various sports as an indicator of the dominant activities in the community.

Transportation and Traffic Patterns

Identifying Transportation Patterns

Current transportation patterns have either preceded or succeeded development of the community. A community analysis must determine how traffic patterns are constructed, or whether the traffic patterns controlled by the design of the community. This is a fundamental consideration.

The location of a library and the surrounding traffic patterns can influence access to and use of the library, along with the hours and delivery of library and information services. The following questions are pertinent:

- To what extent do traffic patterns influence the behavior of community residents?
- What means of public transportation are available? Is there an adequate public transportation system? How accessible is public transportation in each neighborhood?
- *To what extent are local traffic patterns extensions of regional or statewide conditions?* How independent are they?
- What groups are most affected by traffic patterns, barriers, and changes?
- What are plans for future development of public transportation and highways?
- How do people get from one place to another? During what times of the day do they travel?
- Is the library or information center conveniently located?

- Do library hours coincide with transportation and work patterns?
- How do people get to work?

Sources of Information about Traffic Patterns

Traffic pattern information can be attained by driving and walking around, consulting the local security office or police department, or contacting the planning department of the community.

Communication

Identifying Communication Patterns

The communication systems of a community are components of the community's knowledge infrastructure, as discussed in Chapter 3. The library is a vital component in this infrastructure, and studying the communication systems is important in this analysis.

Communication issues are among the most dynamic issues in society today. Technologies that have developed in the last decades have changed patterns of communication, from highly sophisticated urban communities to rural areas. Forms of communication include one-way and two-way media, with newspapers, radio, and television media working primarily in a one-way direction. Recent technologies have enhanced two-way communication. These technologies include everything from global positioning systems to iPods and Internet wikis. Cell phones, the Internet, and computer networks have contributed to the development of blogs, and a community analysis should include an assessment of the presence of blogs and web sites within the community, and the extent to which residents may access them. A library could easily offer courses of instruction on how to write a blog and create a network, serving as a resource to enhance networking. Social networking systems are becoming powerful communication devices within a community.

Investigating communication infrastructure and communication patterns in a community is begun by addressing the following questions:

- Is the communication infrastructure supportive of easy and frequent communication among the community residents? Are there blockages to effective communication?
- What is the qualitative level of opinion leadership provided by mass communication agencies?
- How many radio/public television/cable stations are there and what kind of programming do they offer? Do these stations make available free broadcast time for educational programs or forthcoming events of community interest? What is the estimated audience of these stations?

- What news publications are available in the community, such as newspapers, industrial newsletters, penny savers, and other publications?
- What means of communication exist at the neighborhood or town level?
- What is the interest in national and international events, issues, etc.?
- What less formal sources of communication are in the area? Who are the opinion leaders? How do people get information about the community? What sources do residents use?
- What are the best ways to publicize the library?
- Is there an intersection between the systems for information transfer and knowledge transfer?

Technology Influences on Communication

Communication patterns have been changed remarkably by technology. With each new invention, previous communication technologies and their uses have been modified, but older technologies typically remain. For example, radio did not supplant newspapers, but radio became a news and entertainment medium in addition to newspapers and magazines. Television, which some people said would replace radio, transformed the news reporting and entertainment of radio and newspapers, forcing those media to also change.

More recently, the Internet has impinged on newspapers, magazines, radio, and television, providing more immediacy as well as interactivity among audience members. As a result, newspapers, radio stations, and television stations now have web sites to provide additional news and analysis, allowing for greater consumer reaction. As technology improves, books, periodicals, movies, radio, and television programming are becoming available on the Internet through portable devices such as handheld phones and palmtop computers.

E-mail has speeded up personal communications, enabling people continents apart to communicate in writing almost instantaneously, with the growing capability of transmitting voice over the Internet. Cell phones are ubiquitous, available in most countries in all but the most remote areas. With the capability of cell phones to access the Internet, we have a blending of technologies which revolutionizes the communication process.

When studying the communication patterns of a community, the use of these technologies must be considered, for example:

- How is e-mail used to communicate within and outside the community?
- How is the Internet used as a communication device?
- Do people within the community use blogs—if so, for what purposes?

- Is instant messaging a medium used by members of the community? If so, for what purposes?
- How is the library is a medium for two-way communication as an on-demand service?

Sources of Information about Communication

Information about a community's communication patterns can be collected in the following ways:

- Identify the number and types of radio stations in the community. The library should collect the public documents submitted by the radio station to the Federal Communication Commission. This report indicates the intended audience, meaningful for a public library.
- Scan the various types of newspapers available in the community. Are large metropolitain dailies, smaller local newspapers, penny savers, and commercial newspapers offered? Are there interactive components, blogs, or other opportunities for interaction?
- Determine the number and scope of television stations in the area, including broadcast and cable.
- Interview opinion leaders in the community.
- Browse web sites sponsored by local government and the local chamber of commerce or tourist bureau.
- Search the Internet to determine the online presence of municipal government, the chamber of commerce, and other vital agencies.

Community-ness

As noted earlier, the presence of organized groups within the community is an indication of a level of community-ness, that people in the community like to do things with other people of similar interests. Is there glue that holds the entire community together with a common perception? Bedroom communities often do not have such a common perception. Is the community one in which people care about each other as opposed to those that are uncaring and unaware? Are there neighborhood associations that attempt to make a community attractive and safe for residents?

In urban areas during the twenty-first century, people are moving into suburban residential areas and may become familiar with the residents on both sides of their houses and perhaps across the street, and that may be the extent of their neighborliness. Likewise, those living in large apartment buildings or condominiums may have the same experience, or even less. There may be no feeling of a community at all. People remain isolated from each other and from their communities. Is this the type of community to which you provide library and information service?

Elements of Community-ness

The following questions are pertinent to municipalities but can be adapted to any community, whether school, college/university, or private enterprise.

- Is there a sense of community? Do the community members see themselves as a part of this community? To what extent is there community pride?
- What is the sum total of the community lifestyle? What makes it tick? What makes it unique from the next or any other town, and how great is that difference? What is the dominant culture in the community?
- What are the various subcultures that are influential in the community?
- What is the implication of group activities within the community on a library service's collection or programming?
- What are the level, intensity, and influence of the political activities of these groups?
- Does the available housing determine who lives in the community?
- What activities and interests appear to play dominant roles in the community?
- What pattern of library service is most appropriate for your community?
- Economic life: How would you characterize the economic level of residents? Is the community affluent? "Hanging on" economically? How does the economic condition affect lifestyle?
- Social issues: What are the dominant social concerns of the community members? What issues appear to hold their attention at the present time?
- What kind of cooperative ventures are present in neighborhoods, e.g., neighborhood watches, annual neighborhood events, or other activities that bring people in the area together?
- What makes the community unique?
- Is there a correlation between the amount of community-ness and the existence of groups?
- What is the sum total of lifestyle?
- How does this information give meaning to the other categories of groups, individuals, and agencies?

Sources of Information about Community-ness

The following data-gathering techniques can be used:

- Meet with various organizations and groups.
- Walk or drive around the community.

- Read the local newspaper.
- Talk with residents, especially opinion leaders.
- Scan the web sites of local government and organizations.
- Contact real estate agents or real estate associations.

Economic Life

Identifying Economic Trends

The economic well-being of a community is vital to its continuance and growth. The history of the community undoubtedly includes the industries and businesses that were founded there early on and that influenced the community culture. A must have reason existed for people to live together in this place and carve out livelihoods. Other industries were attracted to the area to continue its growth. What were these businesses and industries?

Among the questions to address when studying the community's economy are:

- Is the community affluent, or is it "hanging on" economically? Why?
- Are workers primarily blue collar or white collar (data available from the census)?
- What is the relationship of factories and places of business to homes?
- Where do people work? To what extent do people commute to other cities?
- What is the cost of homes? Are they affordable to most residents?
- Are taxes high for property?
- Is the library well funded?
- How does the economic condition affect lifestyle?

Sources of Information about Economic Trends

Much information regarding economic trends in a community can be found in census data, as noted in Chapter 6. Census data provide information concerning employment, occupations, industries, and driving time to work. This information is helpful in constructing an economic profile of a community. The most comprehensive and accurate information about residents of the United States is available through the U.S. Census Bureau at its web site, http://www.census.gov/index.html. This U.S. government agency and service provides current data based on the most recent decennial census, sometimes augmented with updated census information or estimates.

The U.S. Census Bureau's *American FactFinder* (http://factfinder.census .gov/home/saff/main.html?_lang=en) enables the user to identify geographic areas by city, county, legislative district, and census tract. By using one or a combination of these areas, the user can obtain census data regarding employment, education, income, housing, economics, trade, business, and much more.

One of the tools in *American FactFinder* is *State and County QuickFacts* (http://quickfacts.census.gov/qfd/). This web site enables readers to gather demographic data about their state and compare those data to national averages for such variables as general population, ethnic population, household income, travel time to work, and economic indicators. County and city data are compared to state data by category. The comparative data are especially valuable for detecting unique or outstanding factors in a community. It offers quick, easy access to census facts about people, businesses, and geography. The home page provides a map of the United States; click on your state to access counties and cities. Data are available on individuals (e.g., ethnic groups, age, education), housing, business (e.g., nonfarm employment, business ownership by ethnicity, sales volume), households (income, percent below the poverty level), and geography (land area, population per square mile). Other online sources of economic data include the following:

- *Statistical Abstract of the United States* (http://www.census.gov /compendia/statab
- *State and Metropolitan Area Data Book* (http://www.census.gov /compendia/smadb/)
- FedStats (http://www.fedstats.gov/)

Each of these information sources is described in more depth in Chapter 6.

Additional data can be gathered about economic conditions using the following techniques:

- Walk or drive around the community
- Read the local newspaper; skim the classified ads
- Talk with residents, especially long-time residents
- Scan web sites for local government and organizations

Social Issues

Identifying Social Issues

What are the dominant social concerns of the community members? What issues appear to hold their attention at the present time? These issues could include some of the following:

- Abortion rights, euthanasia, family planning
  - Affirmative action, gay rights, veterans' rights, women's rights

o Capital punishment, crime prevention, police, prison reform, public safety, shoplifting

o Conservation, carpooling, energy, nuclear energy, offshore drilling, pollution control, recycling, solar energy, space program

o Divorce, marriage, child abuse, foster parenthood, adoption, pet care

o Drinking age, drug abuse, drunk driving

o Exports/imports, foreign aid

o Fair housing, education, literacy

o Freedom of the press, gun control, immigration, legalized gambling

• Health care, alcoholism, birth defects, cancer research, mental health, nutrition, physical fitness, sexually transmitted diseases, smoking

o Mass transportation, product safety, urban planning, minimum wage, tax reform

o Peace

o Religion, prayer in schools

Sources of Information about Social Issues

Additional data can be gathered about social issues using the following techniques:

• Walk or drive around the community
• Read the local newspaper; skim the classified ads
• Talk with residents, especially long-time residents
• Scan the web sites of local government and organizations

SUMMARY

A number of factors combine to form a community's lifestyle. These elements make the community unique; there can be no other community exactly like it. Lifestyle is a composite of a community's history, its concerns and values, customs, topography and climate, leisure activities, transportation and travel patterns, communication infrastructure, economic life, social issues, and its community-ness or sense of community—together these characteristics comprise the lifestyle of a community. Given this distinctive lifestyle, what pattern of library service is most appropriate to a community? What can the groups and agencies do for the library to provide an information infrastructure for this lifestyle? Most of the other evidence in the community analysis process is much harder evidence, and lifestyle data are not. These data are more subjective. The wider the input from members of the community, the more meaningful the conclusions will be. How can a library complement the existing community information infrastructure?

A community's lifestyle is multi-faceted and complex; furthermore, it is dynamic. As new people move in and other residents move out or die, the composition and lifestyle of the community will change. External forces such as storms, earthquakes, floods, economic downturns or booms, new industries, and either population growth or decline change a community's lifestyle. As a result, a community analysis must be updated continuously to monitor these changes, and library and information services must never be static.

REFERENCES

FedStats. http://www.fedstats.gov/ (accessed November 2, 2009).

U.S. Census Bureau. http://www.census.gov/index.html (accessed November 2, 2009).

———. *American factfinder.* http://factfinder.census.gov/ (accessed November 2, 2009).

———. *State and county quickfacts.* http://quickfacts.census.gov/qfd/ (accessed November 2, 2009).

———. *State and metropolitan area data book: 2006.* http://www.census.gov/compendia/smadb/ (accessed November 2, 2009).

———. *The 2010 Statistical Abstract: The National Data Book.* http://www.census.gov/compendia/statab (accessed March 1, 2010).

———. U.S. Department of Commerce. Economics and Statistics Administration. *County and city data book: 2007.* http://www.census.gov/prod/2008pubs/07ccdb/ccdb-07.pdf (accessed March 1, 2010).

CHAPTER 10

Implementing a Community Analysis

CHAPTER OVERVIEW

In this chapter, illustrations using the four perspectives of community analysis are applied to public, school, academic, and special libraries. Ways of organizing staff for collecting data and converting data into decisions are described. When evidence is collected about a community, the result is a static snapshot of a dynamic environment. This snapshot is used to infer the community's needs for information; consequently, it is important to know the kinds of information that community members can access in the library. A significant part of a community analysis is an analysis of library resources available to the community at that time.

An analysis of the library collection and an analysis of the library registration file can be compared with census data to determine who uses the library, who does not, and where users and non-users live. These library analysis techniques are discussed in detail, and a case study is introduced.

ORGANIZING TO GATHER DATA

The previous four chapters outlined the data that should be collected in a community analysis: data on individuals, groups, agencies, and lifestyles and where to find such data. We now investigate **how** to collect the necessary data in order to assess and plan library services. In this section we will explore who should be involved in data collection, and why.

Whom to Involve

We strongly recommend that the people who should collect information about a community should be those who live and work in the community. These people will best understand the data and be able to interpret it for the library. The numbers will have meaning to them.

Each department in the library should be involved. Ideally, a team of one professional and one paraprofessional should work together collecting and analyzing data. In addition to building a closer relationship, this arrangement enables the merging of both professional and paraprofessional perspectives in the planning, implementation, and analysis of data collection. The professional has responsibility for the "big picture" of library services, while the paraprofessional understands the daily operations that enable the effective implementation of services. Ideally, both are members of the library's constituent community.

The staff designated to collect and analyze data should meet initially with the project director (the director of the library or an assistant or associate director) who provides leadership for the project. The project leader must have the authority to make critical decisions for the project, and the project leader must have the "big picture" of the library in mind when making these decisions. Authority and knowledge of the system are very important in assuring project success.

The first meeting of the project staff must include the rationale for the project, or why this project is important. For example, we the authors offered an introductory workshop for the Rangeview Library District (Colorado) in August 2008 as the community analysis workshop was initiated. The workshop began with the director reviewing the recent past for the district, future directions, and where the community analysis fit into these plans. The director addressed the question "Why should we do this when we're already very busy?" **before** other questions were asked. A community analysis is something new, and staff who have been in the system many years think they already know the information needs of clientele. So, why bother? The director also pointed out that only 10 percent of the population uses the library and there is much room for the improvement of services to meet the needs of new clientele. But which services should be offered? This community analysis will help the system staff to decide (1) which services to implement, (2) which current services could be discontinued, and (3) what marketing strategies can be used to target specific audiences.

Organizing into Teams

Data collection staff should be divided into four to six teams in order to collect data on each of the four perspectives in the community analysis model and investigate trends in library use. The teams and types of data to collect are listed here:

- Individuals: census data
- Groups: intuitive data, impressions, systematic data from newspapers and web sites
- Agencies: intuitive data, impressions, systematic data from phone books, directories, and web sites
- Lifestyles: intuitive data, impressions, systematic data from newspapers, oral and written histories, and web sites
- Mapping library user data: maps for users to place pins where they live, circulation and registration information
- Collection data: information from the integrated library system

At the initial meeting, the project director should ask for volunteers for each team or appoint members as necessary. Whenever possible, each team should be headed by a professional with one (or two) staff members to assist. The director should be sure that team membership and timelines decided on at the meeting are recorded for future reference. This same information should be posted on the library's web site so all can follow the project's progress.

The project director and teams should set a reasonable calendar with meetings planned at regular intervals to share successes and losses, discoveries and problems. Such short discussions keep the team focused, maintain momentum and interest, and provide opportunities for problem-solving. The meetings should be short (no more than an hour), organized (have an agenda), and be open for sharing of feelings as well as actions. The data-gathering process can be laborious, and such meetings can boost teams' morale. As with the initial meeting, the project director should chair these meetings and be certain that summaries are written and posted for all to see.

COMMUNITY ANALYSIS

Collecting Data on Individuals, Groups, Agencies, and Lifestyles

Detailed instructions and rationale for collecting data are found in Chapters 6–9. Following is a brief summary of key ideas from those chapters.

Individuals

See Chapter 6 for an in-depth discussion on gathering data for individuals. As we consider the information needs of individuals and design information services, we must consider how individuals become aware of an information need, decide to act on that need (or not), implement strategies in searching for information, display preferences for certain formats of media, assimilate the information using a unique cognitive or learning style, and organize, store, retrieve, and use information. A careful information interview can determine the client's approaches and preferences for information format.

These principles are important to apply as data are gathered and services planned for individuals. Sources of information about individuals in a community include government census data and other public sources, most of which are accessible via the Internet. Several federal web sites are fruitful sources of demographic information. We recommend the use of existing data, rather than conducting a new survey, whenever possible. Additionally, other agencies in the community may have recently conducted or commissioned surveys that could provide useful information.

Groups

See Chapter 7 for more information about defining groups and collecting data. Because groups are informal, identifying groups in a community can be challenging. Newspapers within the community are a good source of information for identifying groups, clubs, and various organizations. So, too, are local radio stations, as they may regularly broadcast the meeting times and places of various community groups. Directories may be available in print or on web pages. Groups may have newsletters, perhaps in electronic format. Many groups have a web site, and this source can be effective in making contact, and study of the web site can help determine the group's information needs.

Another good source is people in the community; talk with community residents to determine which are the most popular clubs and other organizations. From these random conversations will arise a general understanding of the names, relative popularity, and activity of groups within the community. Still another fruitful source is bulletin boards scattered throughout the community. Make it a point to walk around and study bulletin boards; take note of groups and their activities, as well as contact information.

The best place to begin gathering data about groups in a municipality is the local newspaper (either online or in print). Read carefully every item in the newspaper on a daily basis for a week, perhaps twice if it is a weekly publication. Include in your analysis the news items, obituaries (noting local organizations mentioned), classified ads, and editorials. Every item is a potential source of information. We suggest creating a matrix like that in Figure 7.1 to record the trends that you observe, including especially favored meeting days.

Agencies

Chapter 8 discusses agencies in detail. Because they are formal organizations, the local telephone directory is a good source for identifying agencies.

The sources of information for agencies are similar to that of groups. Walk-arounds (or drive-arounds), newspapers, especially the yellow pages of the phone book, directories, and people in the community are all good sources of information regarding the dominant and most active agencies in the community. Because the Internet is now a ubiquitous source of information, a "virtual tour" of a community can be very informative.

However, we advise the reader to take a systematic approach to discovering agencies by following a procedure similar to that of identifying groups:

1. Create categories.
2. Collect rough estimates of the number of agencies in each category.
3. Refine those estimates when you need more information to choose among services that can be offered.

Additional information on an agency can be gleaned by examining the mission statement and objectives of the agency, annual reports, newsletters, and marketing publications.

Lifestyles

As discussed in Chapter 9, a number of factors combine to form a community lifestyle. These elements make the community unique. Lifestyle is a composite of a community's history, its concerns and values, customs, topography and climate, leisure activities, transportation and travel patterns, communication infrastructure, economic life, social issues, and community-ness or sense of community. Together these comprise the lifestyle of a community.

A community's lifestyle is multi-faceted and complex; furthermore, it is dynamic. As new people move in and other residents move out or die, the composition and lifestyle change. External forces such as storms, earthquakes, floods, economic downturns or booms, new industries, and either population growth or decline change the lifestyle. As a result, a community analysis must be updated continuously to monitor these changes, and library and information services must never be static.

Briefly, information regarding a community's lifestyle can be gleaned from the following sources:

- Reading histories, reports, newspapers, and documents of the community found in libraries, local museums, archives, and public records
- Talking with longtime residents of the community
- Visiting local park and recreation agencies and interviewing staff
- Reviewing telephone directories

- Visiting local stores and hobby shops
- Perusing local government and chamber of commerce web sites.
- Driving or walking around the community
- Consulting the police department
- Interviewing opinion leaders in the community
- Meeting with various organizations and groups
- Contacting real estate agents or real estate associations
- Mapping demographic and library use data

Library Resource Analysis

Map Study

While teams of staff members are collecting data on the community outside the library, other staff teams should be collecting data on current users and the library collection. An analysis of current users can be done easily by posting a map of the service area and asking clientele to put stick pins where they live. The time period for such a study should be commensurate with one loan period.

Also, pull data from users' registration records. From the map and library records, attempt to answer the following questions (**as many as feasible**):

- Who uses the library?
- What is the proportion of library users to non-users?
- How does the library address the needs of current library users?
- What is the profile (demographics and lifestyle) of your library users from within one mile of the library's location?
- How does this library user profile differ as their distance from the library increases?
- How are elderly library users distributed relative to the library's location?
- How are the ethnic and immigrant library user populations distributed relative to the library's location?
- How are children and young adult library users distributed relative to the library's location?
- How are physically disabled library users distributed relative to the library's location?
- How are other "special" and traditionally under-served library users distributed relative to the library's location?
- How accessible is the library via public transportation services relative to library service hours?
- How do topographical features, such as public highways and rivers, influence the access and use of library services?

- What competitors exist in the area (other libraries, bookstores, and information services)?
- Who doesn't use the library, and why?

The validity of findings from this map study and interviews can be checked by sampling the registration file. Post this sample on a map which indicates various census tracts to see the distribution of clientele. The registration file analysis process is described below.

Today, Geographic Information System (GIS) software is used to present census information in a map-based form. The GeoLib Database (http://www.geolib.org/PLGDB.cfm), and Civic Technologies (http://www.civic technologies.com/library/index.cfm), for example, combine census information, public library use data, and other publicly available information from more than 16,000 public library locations in the United States. The resulting maps help public libraries adjust their tactics to better respond to the needs of their constituencies. Browse tutorials for these software programs and assess their usefulness for analyzing your community.

Registration File Analysis

The single most important file in the library is the registration file, not the shelf list. If a library should burn down, the registered borrowers will likely be the prime movers to rebuild it. The registration must be updated often so that the number of children and adults registered as borrowers is current. The registration file should demand a great deal of attention to keep it vital. Any establishment that has a complete list of its client population has unbelievable good fortune, because they know the people who are interested in their service and value it. Businesses value their customers. The registration process is the single most important interaction between the client and the library. It determines how that person feels about the library. Among the vital questions in assessing the validity of a registration file are:

- How often is the registration file updated?
- How many adults are still registered as children?
- What is the relationship between the registration file and the data plotted on a map showing census tracts?

Because they are most knowledgeable about the community, a group of senior citizens may be invited to plot the registration file sample on the map, indicating the locations of users. This use study provides a comprehensive view of which registered clients actually use the library, and where they live.

How large should this sample be? In general, and quite simply, the larger it is, the better it is. According to Powell (2004, 107), an appropriate and generalizable sample size for a population of up to one million books would be 400 users. (See Powell for a readable and thoughtful discussion of sampling and sampling sizes.)

These data, combined with data on library traffic during a week-long period, help to flesh out meaning from the registration file sample and the use study. Ideally, separate samples of adults and children provide a more detailed picture, if the community is large enough.

Shelf List Study

A shelf list is the file that lists titles as books and other media appear on the shelf in the library's collection. While the term is used less often today, we call attention to this source of information that is part of the library's integrated information system.

Using the library's information system, we suggest a sample of 400 titles to assure a large enough sample for generalizing to the entire collection. By having a large sample, you can generalize sufficiently. Having cells of 10 (each cell being a Dewey classification category) enables generalization to the whole.

The following questions can be addressed by this analysis (as many as feasible):

- How old are the titles (by subject area, fiction/non-fiction, user population, etc.)? Note the value of print resources in different subjects relative to their age, e.g., technology versus humanities.
- How much use is made of the collection? Calculate the use factor by dividing the circulation percentage of the subject area by the holdings percentage of the same subject. A use factor of 1.0 indicates a balance between acquisition and use.
- What proportion (subject area, genre, or user focus) of the sample receives the greatest proportion of use? How do the unique characteristics of this collection (e.g., age and size) and user population affect the 80/20 rule, i.e., 20 percent of the collection accounting for 80 percent of what is circulated?
- How many titles are lost (to theft or non-return of titles)? Percent of loss is the number of titles not found compared to the total number of titles checked in the sample. In a broader approach, the shelf availability study would examine the reasons for which customers are unable to locate the items they are looking for when they visit the library.
- How accurately does the catalog reflect the shelf list (i.e., correctly identifying an item's bibliographic citations, location, availability, etc)? In an integrated library system, this should not be a problem.

- What titles have multiple copies and how adequate are the multiple copies relative to demand as reflected by use patterns?
- How much interlibrary borrowing is done to supplement this collection sample?
- How much use of the items is done in-house as compared to circulation use, if sample is monitored longitudinally?
- How do the online resources subscribed to by the library supplement this sample collection?
- How does this sample collection support the library's reference and web site resources, and relate to the social networking technologies used in the community?

WHAT DO THE NUMBERS MEAN?

A community analysis, properly done, results in a large amount of data collected from and relating to individuals, groups, agencies, and lifestyles of the library's clientele. Also collected are data regarding the existing collection and existing registered clientele. What is the meaning of all this data? We offer below a brief explanation for data collected for public, school, academic, and special libraries and information centers. In Chapter 12, we provide specific directions for using this information in planning information services.

Public Libraries

See Chapters 6–9 for more detailed instructions for gathering data on individuals, groups, agencies, and lifestyles for the service areas of public libraries. Additionally, we offer suggestions in those chapters that pertain specifically to public libraries and their service areas.

When assembling data on individuals, librarians should have at least ten sample subjects in each of the census districts in order to generalize to the population in your service area. We suggest plotting a random sample from the registration file on a map to see proportion registered and not registered (see "Registration File Analysis" above for more specific directions). Separating out adults and children, provide data on who is using the library and who is not. The area around the library tends to be concentrated with dots; the further away from the library, the sparser tends to be the use of the library. This analysis shows what geographical and topographical features inhibit library use, e.g., interstate highways, rivers, or other land features. A river does the same thing as an old bridge—in one community it was discovered that kids would not use the library because their parents would not let them traverse the old, dangerous bridge between the residential area and the library located directly across the river.

School Libraries Media Centers

School libraries have a limited clientele: the students, teachers, and administrators working in that school building. The same four perspectives can be used—individuals, groups, agencies, and lifestyles—but most of the data collection can be done in-house within the school environment. Individual student statistics are usually collected and maintained as requirements for local, state, and national reporting. These data are readily available through the principal's office or through the district office.

Information on organized groups within the school is available on the school web site, through groups' sponsors, interviews with student members, and through school counselors. Individual classes may also be counted as groups.

Agencies within the school would include department personnel if the school is large enough and student and faculty services, e.g., nurses, counselors, custodial services, and bus service. The individuals who provide these services can be contacted for more information. Local service agencies may also provide services to a substantial number of students and teachers; these agencies should also be taken into account.

The lifestyle of the general community greatly influences values found within the school. School librarians should take note of the Chapter 9 on lifestyles and the above section on lifestyles to be aware of the unique history, culture, and traditions of the community as well as the lifestyle of the school. The school librarian(s) should take special note of the answers to this question: To what extent are the lifestyles of the school and community similar or different? Understanding the culture within a school and molding the library to be compatible with it is an important goal.

Universities and Colleges

A college or university community analysis, like that of a school library media center, is less complex than that of a public library. The library clientele are more easily defined and contacted. For example, the educational needs of faculty can be identified by collecting syllabi each semester and checking the reading lists on the syllabi to ensure that the library has an adequate number of copies for the works cited, so that the library is supporting the courses. In addition, the library staff can collect curricula vitae from the faculty and note the areas taught and researched to pinpoint subject areas the faculty are engaged in. This information can provide valuable input on materials selection and evaluations of potential selections. Libraries serve students best with educational services when also serving the faculty.

The college or university library can develop a customized process for supporting faculty research. The library could order a book and send it to a faculty member to say that he or she has three days (or any specified period of time) to let the librarians know whether to keep the book or send it back. We suggest that faculty members should be encouraged to create three lists—(1) resources that they "must have," (2) titles they would like to have but that are not critical, and (3) a wish list of resources that would be useful. Such lists can be reviewed by professional staff to provide guidance on what faculty think is essential.

Librarians in academic libraries can customize more easily than in public libraries, because they can know exactly what faculty and students' educational and research needs are. However, academic librarians must ask the question, "Are we going to support informational and recreational needs as well as educational?" This question is usually addressed from a pragmatic perspective—can the library afford to address informational and recreational needs if those needs are not central to the university's and library's missions? What services will be offered to students and to faculty? Will graduate students receive a different level of service than undergraduate students?

The academic community analysis must make certain that the library is part of the academic program instead of apart from it; to do this, librarians must know the academic programs at their university and what is important in faculty and students' lives.

Special Libraries

Special libraries, like school and academic libraries, serve a defined clientele; consequently, information professionals in corporate or other types of special libraries can interview each member of the agency to identify specific information needs. Also, without intruding on privacy, the information professional can collect the resumes of key people in the organization conducting research or making decisions so that the library information center can customize the selection and use policies to fit clientele needs.

As suggested for public libraries, special libraries and information centers should study their registration files and their collections and synthesize the results with the data collected from the analysis of their community. This comparison will help the information professional to see where changes should be made in selection and use policies.

CASE STUDY

In late spring of 2008, an agreement was reached between the authors of this book and leadership of the Rangeview Library District near Denver, Colorado to collaborate in conducting a community analysis for the district. In exchange for providing access to data collected and for permission to interview library district personnel, the authors agreed to conduct a workshop in summer 2008, and serve as consultants during the project. The following is a description of the workshop and the data collection techniques that were employed.

Introduction to the Library District

The Rangeview Library District (RLD) serves all residents of Adams County except the cities of Aurora and Westminster, and Deer Trail School District; these communities are served by libraries that existed before the establishment of RLD. The Rangeview Library District provides library and information services through six branch libraries and through its Outreach Services Division, which operates a bookmobile and offers services to homebound residents.

The library district encompasses 1,200 square miles north of the city of Denver. RLD serves a diverse population in the rural towns of Bennett and Strasburg and the cities of Brighton, Commerce City, Federal Heights, Northglenn, and Thornton, as well as in all unincorporated areas of the county. Many people work outside the district service area but live in the district.

The Rangeview Library District became operational and independent of the Adams County government in January 2008. The Adams County Board of County Commissioners appointed the five-member Library Board of Trustees that oversaw the operation of RLD. A new director and associate director were hired in late 2007, and immediately began to plan for and implement plans for expanded library services.

According to library district leaders, library branch directors and staff know only about the people who use their libraries. One manager noted that circulation was going up, but she had no idea why; she didn't know who used the library and who didn't. The district leadership wanted to create an infrastructure and a philosophy of library service that was customer-centered. There was no prevailing philosophy of service in the district when the workshop was conducted.

The Workshop

A half-day workshop was planned for early August. The objective was to provide for each branch manager and one staff member from each branch the philosophy and data collection techniques needed to conduct a useful community analysis. Workshop participants included all six branch directors, branch staff members assigned to collect data, system-wide administrators, and a graduate student intern assigned to the project, a total of 20 people.

Before the workshop, participants were asked to read a chapter on community analysis in the authors' book *Introduction to the Library and Information*

Professions (2007). Participants were asked to bring to the workshop the following items:

- Census tract data for their service areas. Workshop leaders identified key categories of data and discussed the meaning of the variables relevant to their decision-making, and why that information is important.
- Local telephone books, local newspapers, and penny savers. These information sources are used to identify agencies—go to the yellow pages and newspapers to see what kinds of businesses are dominant.
- Laptops were not available at the workshop to check local government and chamber of commerce Internet sites. Unfortunately, the wi-fi system at the workshop site was also unavailable. Instead, participants were asked to view these web sites before the workshop.
- Data on the number of adults and children registered to use each library.

The workshop began with the library district director providing a rationale for conducting a community analysis, or why it was important to the library distract. The goal of the district is to have libraries that serve people, not just store books.

The workshop leaders then asked attendees to introduce themselves by answering the following questions: (1) What makes your library unique? (2) How is your library perceived in the community? (3) How valuable is the library in the community? Answers included the following diverse observations:

- The library is "tucked away." People don't know where we are.
- The library is loved, appreciated, and respected.
- People are not literate and do not know the library's value.
- The library is valuable to long-term residents but not to transients.
- Libraries provide literacy education and other outreach, but "they are full," i.e., the library space is inadequate for the number of regular clientele.
- It's a place to hang out and use computers.
- We have outstanding programming for children and teens.
- They [clients] "suck up what we offer." Our programs are always well attended.
- We have an opportunity to redevelop and change our identity. We have a long way to go to meet the needs of the entire community.
- The most rural branch was described as "the adhesive that holds the community together."
- Ninety percent of the residents do not use the library.

- The staff is excellent! We are still working on learning how the community perceives us.
- The population is changing. We work to give patrons (new residents to the U.S.) "a leg up."
- We've got the resources and the vision to serve 5–10 times more people than we now serve.
- The blue collar residents are shocked we are there. We have reached out to the white collar community and been received well. It's a challenge to serve both.

In summary, one could say that staff members generally believe that their library has done a good job serving clientele. Still others perceive the need to do a better job serving their community, and one of the participants revealed (and this was supported by the library district leaders) that approximately 10 percent of the Adams County population is served by libraries. Who are the 90 percent who go unserved, and what are their needs?

The workshop leaders emphasized that a well-selected and well-maintained collection doesn't say much about what a library does. The participants were urged to think of the library as an information utility. An information needs assessment is essential, and the first step toward becoming an information utility, a vital information source for citizens, local government, the private sector, and public organizations.

Next, participants were asked, "Who uses the library? Who doesn't? Why?" Following are a sample of the reasons given for residents *not* using libraries:

- People can't find us.
- The library has old technology.
- We don't fulfill their needs.
- There is a lack of targeted marketing.
- Sometimes people really don't care.
- People have high fines or have lost books.
- Schools and neighborhoods can't get to the library.
- The library's reputation (obviously a bad one!).
- People feel intimidated by the library.
- There is a language barrier between the library and the community.

Participants were urged to return to their libraries with this assignment:

1. Each person on the staff should take one group of people, look at the census data, and compare the list of census categories with the number of people in each of the census categories listed in the registration file.
2. Staff members should note the types of materials checked out by each census data group.

3. Participants were encouraged to post a map of their service area and ask everyone who came in to put a pin in the map to show where they live. At the end of a loan period, library staff would be able to see their service area from the pattern formed by the pins.

Data-gathering techniques were described: intuitive, impressionistic, systematic, and scientific (see Chapter 7). Participants were encouraged to value their experiences on a daily basis. They know a great deal about their communities and should use that knowledge. Outside consultants can't know these things.

The community analysis model was described: groups, agencies, individuals, and lifestyles (see Chapters 5 and 6–9). These terms were defined briefly, along with techniques for gathering each type of data. The process of converting findings into services was also outlined.

Workshop leaders urged each branch staff to form teams of four (one team each for individuals, groups, agencies, and lifestyles) to gather data. They were asked to meet at least once each month to share impressions and record a summary of their findings. The project intern, a master's degree student at the Emporia State University School of Library and Information Management, served as a resource to answer questions and help with data collection and analysis. The project coordinator was a member of the library district administrative team who could be consulted regularly, and the workshop leaders were also available to answer questions by e-mail and telephone.

The project coordinator announced that she and the intern would meet to determine the next steps, and the project was scheduled to be completed in four months (December). In the meantime, participants were urged to collect information about the library collection and conduct the map study.

The library system director concluded the workshop by reinforcing the importance of library staff collecting data in order to know their communities better. The library system made this community analysis a priority, in addition to building four new libraries, equipping these libraries, and hiring and training library staff. The administrative team wanted to reinvent public libraries, and it began by conducting community analysis. The library system director concluded by recalling that the pioneers who came from the east in their wagons did not let the mountains stop them on their way to California: "If the pioneers could get their wagons over the mountains, we can figure out how to complete this community analysis."

Implementation of the community analysis model and conversion of analysis results into services is discussed in the next chapter.

SUMMARY

In this chapter we provided instructions for using the four perspectives of a community needs analysis as applied to public, school, academic, and special libraries. Using data to make program decisions was discussed. When evidence is collected about the community, it is important to know what kinds of information the community can access in the library. We have described steps for conducting an analysis of library resources available to the community, along with a description of an analysis of the registration file. A map study was suggested in order to determine where library clients reside. These three activities yield information about library effectiveness, including who uses the library, who does not, where clientele live, and which resources appear to address clientele needs.

A case study was introduced in order to demonstrate how a library staff can be organized and introduced to community analysis.

REFERENCES

Greer, Roger C., Robert J. Grover, and Susan G. Fowler. 2007. *Introduction to the library and information professions*. Westport, CT and London: Libraries Unlimited.

Powell, Ronald R. 2004. *Basic research methods for librarians*. 4th ed. Library and Information Science Text Series. Westport, CT and London: Libraries Unlimited.

CHAPTER 11

Extrapolating Meaning from Community Analysis Data

CHAPTER OVERVIEW

After data are collected using the community analysis model, then what? This chapter reviews sources of community information and explains how to extract meaning from this information for customizing new or existing services in libraries and information agencies.

WHAT THE DATA TELL US

Let us now examine data from each of the four perspectives to determine what information we have. We will examine data collected for individuals, groups, agencies, and lifestyles.

INDIVIDUALS

Demographics of a community present a composite view of the individuals in a service area. As noted in Chapter 6, you must first be certain that the service area of the information agency is clearly identified. Often the library service area and the boundaries for census data are not an accurate reflection of individuals served by the library. The following are characteristics that are informative in the analysis of individuals within a population, and which can be attained from recent census data:

- Age characteristics
- Family structure, including households and children, marital status

- Educational characteristics, including school enrollment and years of school completed
- Economic characteristics, including employment status, occupation, industry, and income

The examples above for municipalities can be adapted easily to other kinds of communities as well, as noted in Chapter 6. The communities of colleges, schools, private enterprises, and government agencies also can be analyzed in the same way.

Regardless of the type of community, analysis of **individuals** is intended to break down a complex organization and look at the people who populate that organization. That is the purpose of analyzing the demographics of a community.

Case Study Results

Our case study was introduced in Chapter 10. Teams comprised of a branch head and one staff member each were assisted by the project intern, a student in the master's degree program at the Emporia State University School of Library and Information Management. The intern worked with the project coordinator to assist with data collection, presentation, and analysis. Data were collected from September 2008 through March 2009. Analysis of the data was completed in April and presented to the library district leadership early in May. Data collection included the following activities:

- Information about individuals was gleaned from census data and corroborated with data collected by a regional intergovernmental agency.
- A map study was conducted for each branch. During one loan period, a map of the surrounding area was posted near the circulation desk in each branch, and customers were asked to place a pushpin where they live.
- Phone books and web sites were searched for the names of area groups and agencies.
- A brief questionnaire was made available for two weeks at the circulation desk of each branch library.

One of the book authors interviewed the project coordinator monthly during data collection. Data tables in this section present an overview of each of the six library branches that comprise the Rangeview Library District, renamed in 2009 "Anythink, a Revolution of Rangeview Libraries." After studying the general characteristics of individuals for all six communities to gain a perspective of community differences, we focus on one library branch to study the groups, agencies, and lifestyles in order to plan appropriate library services.

Population

Information about the population and age distribution of the six studied communities is cumulated in Table 11.1.

Thornton, the most populous community, has the largest proportion of adults ages 45–64 and a small percentage of seniors over the age of 65. With a median age of 30.6, Thornton is the second youngest community. Perl Mack and Northglenn have the largest proportion of senior citizens. The residents of Bennett and Commerce City have a low median age and a low percentage of seniors.

Education

Our community analysis research indicated that educational attainment typically is the best indicator of library usage. Educational attainment for residents in library branch communities is cumulated in Appendix A and summarized in Table 11.2. Following are major findings from the census data:

- Perl Mack has the lowest attainment of education; nearly 64 percent have a high school education or less, and 10 percent have a bachelor's or master's degree.
- Commerce City is similar to Perl Mack in that 61 percent have a high school diploma or less, and 16 percent have a bachelor's or master's degree.
- Bennett, Northglenn, and Thornton have high levels of educational attainment; more than half of their residents have some college level education.
- Thornton's residents have achieved the highest level of education. Twenty-four percent have earned a bachelor's or master's degree, and more than half (55.8%) of all residents have at least some college. Only 44.2 percent have a high school diploma or less.
- Northglenn is close behind Thornton in educational attainment. More than half of the residents have some college education and 17.9 percent have a bachelor's or master's degree.
- Brighton, the community chosen for the case study, is near the mean for educational attainment among the six communities. About half (51.5%) of the residents have a high school education or less, and 17.6 percent have a bachelor's or master's degree.

Table 11.1 Population and Age Distribution among Communities.

Communities	Total Population	Median Age	Ages 0–4	Ages 5–9	Ages 10–19	Ages 20–24	Ages 25–44	Ages 45–64	Ages 65+
Bennett	2,581	30.9	9.0%	9.4%	19.0%	4.2%	34.7%	18.1%	5.6%
Brighton	30,654	31.9	9.4%	8.7%	15.7%	5.1%	34.5%	18.1%	8.5%
Commerce City	40,929	30.0	10.8%	9.6%	11.5%	5.0%	39.2%	18.1%	5.8%
Northglenn	36,889	33.5	6.8%	7.1%	12.7%	7.3%	34.2%	21.5%	10.5%
Perl Mack	43,102	31.7	7.6%	7.5%	15.4%	9.1%	30.8%	19.1%	16.6%
Thornton	109,918	30.6	9.5%	8.4%	13.4%	6.5%	34.3%	22.0%	5.8%
Community Mean	44,012	31.4	8.8%	8.5%	14.6%	6.2%	34.6%	19.5%	8.8%

Table 11.2 Educational Attainment for the Six Communities.

Community	High School diploma or less	Some college or Associate's degree	Bachelor's degree	Graduate or professional degree
Bennett	49.3%	38.5%	10.5%	1.8%
Brighton	51.5%	30.9%	11.6%	6.0%
Commerce City	61.0%	22.9%	12.5%	3.6%
Northglenn	49.9%	32.2%	13.7%	4.2%
Perl Mack	64.1%	26.0%	7.0%	3.0%
Thornton	44.2%	31.3%	17.7%	6.8%
Community Mean	53.3%	30.3%	12.2%	4.2%

Racial Trends

Table 11.3 summarizes race-based data for the six communities. Following are key trends:

- Bennett, the smallest community, is the most skewed in race distribution. The population is overwhelmingly white (92.5%) with the smallest Hispanic population (4.5%) of the six communities.
- Commerce City and Perl Mack have the largest Hispanic populations (51.5% and 45.7%, respectively).
- Brighton also has a substantial Hispanic population (39.1%).
- Northglenn and Thornton are identical in both their Hispanic (27.7%) and white (64%) populations.

Table 11.3 Racial Trends in the Six Communities.

Community	Hispanic or Latino	Caucasian	Other Races
Bennett	4.5%	92.5%	3.0%
Brighton	39.1%	58.0%	2.9%
Commerce City	51.5%	40.1%	8.4%
Northglenn	27.7%	64.3%	8.0%
Perl Mack	45.7%	48.2%	6.1%
Thornton	27.7%	64.2%	8.1%

What the Data Mean for Library Services

In the trends analysis in Table 11.4, we can see how the six communities differ in population, education, and racial trends. Implications for service are also indicated. For example, Bennet's population is concentrated in adults of child-rearing age. Consequently, a library should emphasize services for children, parents, and the concerns of young people beginning and advancing in their careers. Programs and resources on parenting, career guidance, homemaking, home buying, and home repairs are among the suggested topics for programs and resources. Although the minority population in Bennett is small, it should not be overlooked. The library might provide programs on different cultures to educate residents on the multicultural society in which they live.

Service implications are noted in Table 11.4 with examples of library services for each of the cities in the Rangeview Library District.

GROUPS

As noted earlier, groups are formed around common interests, and exploration of groups provides a sketch of individuals' interests in the community. The purpose of analyzing groups is to get a sense of the number of people engaged in various activities. The findings can be coordinated with a study of numbers of titles listed under related subject headings in the library catalog and headings for agencies in the local phone directory.

We also note that it is sometimes difficult to determine the difference between an agency and a group. For example, mental health agencies sponsor numerous groups to help people recover from such conditions as loss of a loved one, alcoholism, and drug addiction. The important point to remember is that understanding groups in a community helps a staff to gain an understanding of the diverse interests in a community. The number and type of groups also show the "community-ness" of the community, a measure of lifestyle. The more groups in a community, the more community-ness is indicated.

Unlike an agency, a group usually does not have an office or permanent telephone for contact, but it may have a contact person (a club president or secretary, for example). Examples of groups in a community would be service organizations, service fraternities and sororities, and social clubs. The local newspaper usually includes news of clubs and their meeting schedules.

To identify and analyze groups systematically, it is helpful to categorize them. For example, a matrix might be constructed using these categories: Recreational, social, religious, cultural, school, hobbies, ethnic, age-related, environmental, political, project-oriented, commercial, and vocational/occupational. It is important at this point in the community analysis to collect impressions, not detailed data. The best place to begin gathering data about groups in a municipality is the local newspaper (online or in print).

Table 11.4 Trends from Data Collection on Individuals.

Town	Population Trends	Education Trends	Race Trends	Service Implications
Bennett	• Smallest community (population 2,581) • High population under the age of 19 • Large middle-aged population (ages 25–44) • Smallest population of seniors (5.6%)	• Nearly half (49.1%) have a high school education or less • 12.3% have a bachelor's or master's degree	• Population is overwhelmingly white (92.5%) • Fewest Hispanics (4.5%) of the six communities	• Emphasize services for families & children • Provide educational services to children & middle-aged population • The small Hispanic population should not be overlooked.
Brighton	• Even distribution of all age groups • Has a large number of children and adults of parenting age	• About half (51.5%) have a high school education or less • 17.6% have a bachelor's or master's degree.	• Has a substantial Hispanic population (39.1%)	• Provide services to Hispanic population • Services for all age groups
Commerce City	• Lowest median age (30) and the largest percentage of children under the age of ten • Highest percentage of people of child-rearing ages (25–44)	• 61% have a high school diploma or less • 16% have a bachelor's or master's degree	• With Perl Mack, has the largest Hispanic population (51.5%)	• Emphasize services to children & parents, Hispanic population

(continued)

Town	Population Trends	Education Trends	Race Trends	Service Implications
Northglenn	• Highest median age • Smallest percentage of children below the age of 10	• Half (49.9%) have a high school education or less • 17.9% have a bachelor's or master's degree	• Hispanic population = 27.7% • White population = 64%	• Provide services to the elderly and the Hispanic population
Perl Mack	• Largest proportion of seniors age 65 and older (16.6%)	• Lowest level of educational attainment • 64% have a high school education or less • 10% have a bachelor's or master's degree	• With Commerce City, has the largest Hispanic population (45.7%)	• Provide services to the elderly and the Hispanic population
Thornton	• Most populous community • Largest population of adults age 45–64 • Smallest percentage of seniors over the age of 65 • With a median age of 30.62, Thornton is the second youngest community	• 44.2% have a high school diploma or less • More than half (55.8%) have some college • Only 13.7% of residents have less than a high school diploma • 24% have a bachelor's or master's degree	• Hispanic population = 27.7% • White population = 64%	• Highly educated— provide book & film discussions • Provide directory of learning opportunities in community & nearby

To demonstrate the process for identifying groups, we selected the city of Brighton, Colorado, and consulted the local newspaper online, the Brighton Sentinel Blade (http://www.metrowestfyi.com/farmerminer/links_churches .php). The newspaper lists 43 churches in Brighton, each of which has a number of Bible study and planning groups. The "Groups" section of the newspaper lists the following groups that meet weekly. Although the newspaper lists meeting place and contact information for an individual, we have included below only the group name and meeting days, and we have categorized the groups by the list of topics outlined in Chapter 7.

Age-related
Monday morning coffee, 8 a.m.–noon, Afterglows Senior Center
Tuesday nutrition meal, seniors 60 and older, Afterglows Senior Center
Brighton Senior Center Advisory Board, 1 p.m. 3rd Tuesdays
Potluck, 6–8 p.m. 4th Fridays, Afterglows Senior Center
Video Night, 7 p.m. 2nd Fridays, Afterglows Senior Center
Boy Scout Troop 109, regular meetings 7 p.m. Mondays; boys ages 11–18 and
    their parents are welcome
Boy Scout Troop 193 meets 7 p.m. every Thursday
Cub Scout Pack 391 meets 6:45 p.m. Tuesdays
Boy Scout Troop 315 meets 7 p.m. Tuesdays
Cub Scout Pack 61 meets Tuesdays from 7 to 8 p.m.
Cub Scouts No. 77, Den meetings 7 p.m. Thursdays, Pack meetings 7 p.m.
    4th Thursdays

Church-related
Lorraine Chapter 52 Order of the Eastern Star, 7:30 p.m. 1st and 3rd Tuesdays
Welcome Table (Disciples of Christ) discussion groups, 2:30 and 7:30 p.m.
    Wednesdays
Brighton Masonic Lodge No. 78 AF & AM, 7:30 p.m. 2nd and 4th Thursdays

---

Commercial
None listed

Cultural
Performing Arts Council, 7 p.m. 3rd Mondays
European Music Society Club, 7:30 p.m. 2nd Tuesdays
Brighton Book Club, 10 a.m. 2nd Wednesdays
Platte Valley Players theatre group, 7 p.m. 2nd Wednesdays
Brighton Palette and Brush Club, 9 a.m. 1st Fridays
Daughters of the American Revolution, 1st Saturdays (Sept.–June)
The Territorial Daughters of Colorado, 2nd Saturdays every other month (Sept.–June)
Fifth Sunday Community Sing, 6 p.m.

Environmental
None listed

Ethnic
None listed

Health
Alcoholics Anonymous meets daily [An agency with a permanent location]
Narcotics Anonymous meets Monday and Thursday nights [sponsored by
    an agency]
Overeaters Anonymous meets 7:30 p.m. Tuesdays
Domestic violence support meets 10:30 a.m Wednesdays. Spanish session.
Brighton Al-Anon, 7:45 p.m. Thursdays
Brighton Stroke Group, noon 3rd Thursdays [sponsored by an agency]
Caregivers' Support Group, 10 to 11:30 a.m. 2nd and 4th Thursdays
Pain Management and Fibromyalgia Support Group 7 to 8:30 p.m. 3rd Thursdays
    [sponsored by an agency]
Domestic violence support, 3 p.m Fridays. English session.
Project CASE, suicide grief support, 6 to 8 p.m. 1st and 3rd Wednesdays
    [a program sponsored by an agency]

Hobbies
Brighton Genealogical Society, 7 p.m. the last Monday of the month
Ye Olde Auto Club of Brighton, 2nd Mondays

Political
Brighton Sister Cities group, 5:30 p.m. 4th Mondays

Project-oriented
None listed

Recreation
Story time, 10:30 a.m. and 1:30 p.m. Wednesdays, Rangeview Library Brighton
    branch, ages 3–6
Story time, 10:30 a.m. Fridays, Rangeview Library Brighton branch, ages 3–6
Kids' Nite Out, Fridays, Brighton Recreation Center, ages 8–14

Note: These recreational activities are sponsored by an agency—the local public library and the recreation center.

School

MOPS (Moms with children ages infant–kindergarten), 9–11 a.m. 1st and 3rd
   Tuesdays, Sept.–May
The Mom's Club of Brighton meets every 3rd Wednesday of the month at 10 a.m.
   The group offers fun ways for moms to meet other moms, for the kids to play,
   and for community service projects.
MOPS (Mothers of Preschoolers), 9–11 a.m. 2nd and 4th Thursdays (Sept.–May)
Warm Hearts–Warm Babies, 9 a.m.–2 p.m. 3rd Wednesdays
All-Brighton High School Booster Club, 7 p.m. 3rd Wednesdays

Service Organizations

Brighton Rotary Club, 12:10 p.m. Mondays
Brighton Optimists, 7 p.m. 1st and 3rd Tuesdays
Brighton Early Rotary Club, 7–8 a.m. Wednesdays
Brighton Kiwanis Club meets every Wednesday from noon to 1:00 p.m.
Brighton Breakfast Lions Club, 6:30 a.m. 2nd and 4th Thursdays
Green Valley Grange, 11:30 a.m. 1st Thursdays potluck dinner, 12:30 p.m. meeting.
South Weld Lions Club, 7:30 p.m. 3rd Fridays
South Weld Lions Club, 7:30 a.m. 1st Saturdays
American Legion, 7:30 p.m. 3rd Tuesdays
Brighton Veterans of Foreign Wars Post No. 2841 Ladies' Auxiliary, 7:30 p.m.
   2nd Tuesdays
Brighton Veterans of Foreign Wars Post No. 2841 & Men's Auxiliary, 7:30 p.m.
   2nd Tuesdays.
Philip Wade Post No. 46 American Legion, 6:30 p.m. 1st Thursdays

Social

Women in Touch, 4th Mondays
Open breakfast, 7–11 a.m. 1st Sundays, American Legion Post No. 2002
Veterans of Foreign Wars Men's Auxiliary Post No. 2841 breakfast, 7–11:30 a.m.
   2nd Sundays
Veterans of Foreign Wars Post 2841 breakfast, 7–11:30 a.m. 3rd Sundays
Sunday brunch, 11 a.m.–1 p.m., Inglenook Retirement Center
Mommies at Play, 9:30 a.m. 3rd Thursdays, activity planning

Vocational/occupational

Northern Colorado Woodworkers Association, 2nd Mondays
The Toastmasters Club, Brighton Your Speech, is open to anyone interested in
   learning and practicing communications skills. The club meets the 1st and 3rd
   Tuesday of each month at 11:30 a.m.
Front Range Young Farmers 7 p.m. 2nd and 4th Wednesdays (Sept.–May)

This newspaper list of groups is incomplete, but it presents an impression of the active groups in a community. To flesh out this list, a staff member may call any of these groups' contact people and ask for the names of other groups who do similar things. Also, the library could chart when most people meet; the library could then reduce hours on that evening and/or send a representative to attend meetings to learn about the group's information needs. Communities have a rhythm; for example, residents of a North Carolina town always went fishing on Wednesdays. A certain town in the Midwest is nearly deserted on Wednesday nights because most people are attending church meetings. The spare-time activities of people are indicators of a community's lifestyle.

Studying the types and numbers of groups in the case study suggests the following generalizations for the Brighton community:

- Several groups of young mothers could benefit from programs and resources devoted to parenting young children.
- Because scout troop leaders are volunteers, the scouting group leaders (and leaders of all groups) need information pertaining to leadership and running meetings.
- Scout leaders could benefit from information about the psychological and physical development of children.
- Seniors in the community could be interested in resources on the aging process, good health habits, diet, travel, hobbies, the grieving process, and money management.
- The various health groups could use resources related to their interests—recovery from alcoholism, drug dependency, obesity, etc.
- The presence of various cultural groups suggests a need for a good collection of resources on the arts.

We will return to these tentative findings after analyzing the agencies in the Brighton community.

AGENCIES

Agencies are formal parts of a larger organization, and these agencies provide a service or a product. Agencies are identified and studied for reasons similar to those for the study of groups. For example, a community will have such agencies as a police and fire departments, public library, recreation department, schools, and numerous other agencies with a mission within the municipality. Other types of communities or organizations—schools, colleges or universities, and private or public agencies themselves—have internal agencies as well. A community analysis requires assessing information needs by identifying and analyzing the missions and characteristics of agencies serving the community.

The first challenge is identification of agencies in your community. Because they are formal organizations, a telephone directory is a good source to check first. The sources of information for agencies are similar to that of groups. Walk-arounds (or drive-arounds), newspapers, especially the yellow pages, web sites, directories, and people in the community are all good sources of information regarding the dominant and most active agencies in the community.

While identifying agencies, create categories, collect rough estimates of the number of agencies in each category, and refine those estimates when you need more information to choose between services that can be offered. A good place to start a list of categories is to use the list below, or to consult a telephone directory for your municipality, school, college or university, or private enterprise. In general, agencies may be categorized as follows to create a checklist for a community analysis: government, religious, health care, cultural, educational, business, and informational agencies.

Agencies Case Study

A good place to begin a search for agency information is the city's web site, and Brighton has an informative, current web site (http://www .brightonco.gov/). The city site links to the chamber of commerce site (http://www.brightonchamber.com), which provides a great deal of information on the city. Businesses are listed both by topic and alphabetically. However, there is not a comprehensive list of clubs: only four are listed in the business directory. Using the categories we identified above, we will examine the agencies listed by the chamber of commerce:

Government

Nineteen city departments are listed on the City of Brighton web site, as well as county offices: Board of Commissioners, Economic Development, County Fair, Sheriff, and Workforce and Business Center.

Religious

A directory on the chamber's web page identified 28 churches in Brighton, although the newspaper listed 43.

Health Care

The chamber of commerce web site listed eight health care centers, one audiology clinic, three chiropractic centers, two counseling centers, seven dentists and orthodontists, one hospital, one optometrist/ophthamologist, four pharmacies, and one physical therapy center.

Cultural

One art academy, two dance/performing arts studios, one theater company, and one photography studio were listed by the chamber.

Educational

One art academy (also listed under "cultural"), four colleges, three pre-schools, one private elementary school, one private academy and one public school district with one high school, one middle school, and four elementary schools.

Business

The chamber's business directory listing the categories and number of entries can be found in Appendix B. As one scans this list of businesses, the following generalizations can be made:

- The city has little manufacturing.
- The most numerous agencies are insurance (19), real estate (14), and commercial banks (9).
- Remnants of the city's rural heritage remain: two farm supply stores and a horseback riding stable.
- Information services are prominent: insurance agencies, web design services, real estate agencies, legal services, health services, mortgage services, and financial services.
- The city's recreational facilities include a strong youth program.
- The community has two newspapers: *The Brighton Standard/Blade and Gateway News.*

Recreation

The city provides numerous recreational services through the following agencies: Parks and Recreation Department, Senior Center, Youth Services Department, and Recreation Center. In addition, businesses catering to recreation in Brighton are a golf course, gym and fitness center, and a horseback riding stable.

Implications for Information Services

Two questions for information professionals to consider are (1) which of these agencies could benefit from information services offered by the library, and (2) which information agencies could be partners in offering informaton services to the public? Possible opportunities for library collaboration include the following:

- Working with Youth Services to bring educational, cultural, and recreational resources to youth.
- Partnering with churches to offer services, including language training and acculturation in the Hispanic community.
- Providing cultural services through the educational agencies, especially the art academy, studios, and theatre company.
- Collaborating with the chamber of commerce to provide business information to startup companies as well as smaller companies that lack information professionals and information resources.

LIFESTYLES

The fourth category of our community analysis model is "lifestyles." This term refers to the unique "culture" of the community: its history, values, customs, traditions, topography and climate, leisure activities, and other attributes that make this community unique. These characteristics have an enormous impact on the types of information resources and services required by members of a community.

The elements of a community's lifestyle listed above apply to communities regardless of type, whether a municipality, school, college or university, public agency, or private enterprise. The components of "lifestyle" can influence the types of information services offered in a community of any type.

The four perspectives of a community analysis (individuals, groups, agencies, and lifestyle) will enable the information professional to identify the unique qualities of a community and to identify agencies and groups who are leading contributors to the lifestyle of the community. It is a systematic approach for collecting data for making decisions abut information services to be offered. Lifestyle includes a wide cross-section of any community's heritage and uniqueness.

Lifestyles Case Study

The chamber of commerce web site provides a brief history of the city (see Appendix C). The history of Brighton suggests a city with a rural history that is now merging into the larger Denver metropolitan area. The history explains the agricultural remnants in the business sector (farm supply stores and riding stable). While the history of the city explains a part of the lifestyle or culture of Brighton, a significant impact is also made by the ethnic composition of the city. As indicated by the census data and report of the regional development agency, approximately 40 percent of the population is now Hispanic, and 25 percent of the households speak a language other than English. The tables below show other data that suggest lifestyle characteristics.

The housing data in Tables 11.5 to 11.8 are evidence of an affluent community, with three-fourths of the housing units owner-occupied and a median housing value of $210,000. Furthermore, the median monthly mortgage payment is nearly $2,200. All but 3.6 percent of households have a vehicle, and more than 70 percent have two or more vehicles. Additional information about lifestyle is presented in census data related to patterns of commuting to work, as indicated by the data below.

Table 11.5   Housing Occupancy (2007 statistics).

Total housing units	*10,537*
Occupied housing units	91.02%
Vacant housing units	8.98%
Occupied housing units	*9,591*
Owner-occupied	74.87%
Renter-occupied	25.12%

Table 11.6   Household Value.

Owner-occupied units	*7,181*
Less than $50,000	5.36%
$50,000 to $99,999	1.13%
$100,000 to $149,999	10.6%
$150,000 to $199,999	26.68%
$200,000 to $299,999	40.16%
$300,000 to $499,999	13.94%
$500,000 to $999,999	82.72%
$1,000,000 or more	0%
Median (dollars)	210,000

Table 11.7   Vehicles Available per Household.

Occupied housing units	*9,591*
No vehicle available	3.62%
1 vehicle available	25.22%
2 vehicles available	41.12%
3 or more vehicles available	30.04%

Table 11.8   Mortgage Status and Monthly costs.

Housing units with a mortgage	*5,940*
Monthly Payment	Percent of total
Less than $300	0.88%
$300 to $499	0.89%
$500 to $699	2.15%
$700 to $999	7.63%
$1,000 to $1,499	31.55%
$1,500 to $1,999	30.61%
$2,000 or more	26.3%
Median (dollars)	**$2,171**

Tables 11.9 and 11.10 show the mobility of the Brighton workforce. Approximately one-third of Brighton's workforce (30.4%) lives in Brighton, while one-third (34.2%) of Brighton's residents work in Brighton. This also means that two-thirds of the residents work outside Brighton, and the city could be called a "bedroom suburb." That Brighton is a commuter community is further supported by Table 11.11, which indicates that 75 percent of workers drive to work alone, and the average commute time is 26.4 minutes. Fewer than two percent of local workers live close enough to walk to their work.

Table 11.9   Place of Residence for Brighton's Workforce (Top Ten Rankings).

Place	Number	Percent
Outside of region	3,435	37.4
Brighton	2790	30.4
Unincorporated Adams County	924	10.1
Thornton	614	6.7
Denver	354	3.9
Westminster	314	3.4
Aurora	247	2.7
Northglenn	232	2.5
Lakewood	154	1.7
Unincorporated Jefferson County	115	1.3
Total	**9179**	**100.1**

Table 11.10   Place of Work for Brighton's Residents
(Top Ten Rankings).

Place	Number of Residents	Percent
Brighton	2790	34.3%
Denver	1895	23.3%
Unincorporated Adams County	1075	13.2%
Outside of region	511	6.3%
Commerce City	505	6.2%
Thornton	358	4.4%
Westminster	308	3.8%
Aurora	245	3.0%
Boulder	235	2.9%
Northglenn	213	2.6%
Total	8135	100.0

Table 11.11   Residents Commuting to Work.

Commuting Pattern	Extent
Workers 16 years of age and over	*14162*
Car, truck, or van — drove alone	74.7%
Car, truck, or van — carpooled	18.7%
Public transportation (excluding taxicab)	1.8%
Walked	1.9%
Other means	0.6%
Work from home	2.3%
Mean travel time to work (minutes)	26.4

Lifestyles Summary

Brighton, located in Adams County and northeast of Denver, was founded as an agricultural community, and remnants of the farm and ranching lifestyle remain. According to statistics from the Denver Regional Council of Governments (DRCOG), the population grew by 120 percent between 1980 and 2005 from the 2006 population estimate of 28,065. By 2030, the forecasted population is 52,697, an increase of 88 percent. The city has little manufacturing, and only one-third of the workforce works in Brighton, which supports primarily service occupations with little or no industry.

Workers are accustomed to commuting an average of 26 minutes to work; consequently, it can be presumed that residents would also be willing to hop into their cars and drive moderate distances for library and information services.

The residents are multi-ethnic, with about 38 percent being of Hispanic descent (2000 census), and 11 percent speaking little English. The residents are reasonably well-educated, with 49 percent having attained education beyond high school. Most residents live in single family homes with an average value of more than $200,000. Income level, vehicle ownership, and home ownership all suggest a fairly affluent community that values education. In many ways, Brighton is similar to many newer suburbs of large cities.

MAP CASE STUDY

While teams of staff members are collecting data on the community outside the library, other teams should be collecting data on current users and materials. An analysis of current users can be done easily by posting a map of the service area and asking clientele to stick pushpins where they live. The time period for such a study should be equal to one loan period.

The Brighton map project helped library staff determine who is using the library and where the clients are coming from. Below are key questions, with answers derived from the map study. The responses were attained during an interview with library district leaders Freas and Jones (2009).

- **Who uses the library?** Of the 394 participants in the map study, approximately 6 percent came from the Commerce City/Reunion communities. Of these participants, 115 were children and 279 were adults. There did not appear to be any other towns within Adams County that significantly contributed to Brighton's library usage (Bentfield & Freas 2008). However, the interview supported census data indicating that users include a large population of parents with small children. Other users identified were people without Internet access, retirees, and working adults who use the library for recreational purposes. Most users come from the immediate neighborhood, although some come from Commerce City (13 miles southwest) and Henderson (5 miles southwest).
- **What is the proportion of library users to non-users?** While the library is getting new users, approximately 85 percent of the community are non-users. On opening day for the new branch, the staff gave out hundreds of new library cards.
- **What is the profile (demographics and lifestyle) of library users from within one mile of your library's location?** There are "lots" of

school age children, full-time working adults ages 30–55, and retired residents.

- **How does this library user profile differ as the distance from the library increases?** More distant users include an agricultural population and higher income residents. Surrounding this branch are "rings" of houses of varying ages, houses from the 1950s, newer homes, and agricultural areas. The newer housing has younger families. The village that was Brighton became a city, and it is growing quickly. There is no public transportation.

- **How are senior library users distributed relative to the library's location?** Most seniors live in Brighton, relatively close to the library.

- **How are the ethnic and immigrant library user populations distributed relative to the library's location?** They live closer to the library, while the Caucasian population lives further out.

- **How are physically disabled library users distributed relative to the library's location?** Cannot answer that question. The retired population includes some disabled people, and many are in care facilities that visit periodically. There is one senior residential facility in Brighton. A bookmobile serves rural and less populated areas.

- **How do topographical features such as public highways and rivers influence access and use of library services?** Train tracks are near the library, and some residents are concerned for the safety of children. Also, car traffic is heavy because the library is located on a major east–west street.

- **What competitors exist in the area (other libraries, bookstores, and information services)?** The library has few competitors. A nearby workforce center offers classes on such topics as computer use and writing resumes, but there are no bookstores. The library is the main source for Internet use, and for meetings of boys' and girls' clubs.

- **Who does not use the library, and why?** People who live further away do not use this library. Other non-users are twenty-somethings, high school youth, and people who don't know what the library does. Some school libraries are very good, and this branch works with school libraries, when the school librarians are cooperative. Also, the Hispanic population is not using the library.

- **Other comments.** This library is known for successful children's programming. For example, a new music and movment program filled up an hour after registration opened.

In summary, the map study indicated that most library users are from Brighton, and 30 percent of the users are children. Adult users include parents with small children, retirees, and working adults. Popular library services are Internet use and recreation. While the library is getting new users, approximately 85 percent of the community are non-users. The city has no public transportation for residents who do not have their own transportation. Few disabled people use the library. The busy street and nearby railroad tracks present a possible safety hazard for children. The library provides unique services and meeting rooms for groups. Potential users are people who live at a distance from the library, twenty-somethings, high schoolers, and the Hispanic population. The children's programming already has an expanding clientele.

REGISTRATION FILE CASE STUDY

The most important file in the library is the registration file. The registration file should demand a great deal of attention to keep it vital. The registration process is the single most important interaction between the client and the library—it determines how each person feels about the library. The following questions should be addressed in a study of a library's registration file, and the answers were provided from the Brighton case study.

- **How often is the registration file weeded/updated?** It has not been updated. Staff is waiting for new software as part of the renovation of the library system.
- **How many adults are still registered as children?** No record is kept to differentiate between children and adults. Children and teens cannot have unfiltered access to the Internet, the only difference between adult's and children's services.

In summary, the registration file in this case study is not a reliable source of client information until the old system is replaced.

SHELF LIST DATA CASE STUDY

The Rangeview Library District has used an automated record system for 20 years but will soon convert to a new system. Data are updated each month. Each book has a Radio Frequency Identification (RFID) chip. Inventory can be taken easily by simply passing a wand over books on a shelf. Check-in and check-out is fast.

Libraries with an integrated record system can study the entire collection by requesting specified data. Libraries without such a system might sample the collection instead. We suggest a sample of 400 titles to assure a large enough sample for generalizing to the entire collection. By having a large sample, you can generalize sufficiently. Whether using a random sample or the entire collection, address the questions below. Responses are data from the Brighton branch case study.

- **How old are the titles?** The collection is current. Forty-five percent of the collection was added in 2009; 80 percent of the titles were added in 2007 or later. Only two percent of the collection was added prior to 2005.
- **How much use is made of the collection?** The collection is well used, and usage has increased. The branch has 9,618 adult and 5,546 juvenile active card holders (card holders who checked out materials in the last year). The average monthly circulation for 2009 (through September) was 24,485. The Brighton branch's September circulation was up 21.5 percent from September 2008.
- **What proportion of the collection receives the greatest proportion of use?** Circulation data for September 2009 indicate that adult fiction, children's picture books, and adult nonfiction were the most used.
- **How many titles are lost (to theft or non-return of titles)?** No data are available.
- **How accurately does the catalog reflect the shelf list?** Because it is an automated system, the catalog is an accurate reflection of the shelf list.
- **Which titles have multiple copies, and how adequate are those multiple copies relative to demand as reflected by use patterns?** When there are three holds on a title, a duplicate copy is ordered.
- **How much interlibrary borrowing is done to supplement this collection?** During 2009, the monthly average for interlibrary loan requests was 150. The monthly average for requests filled was 109. With an average circulation of 24,485, interlibrary loan borrowing is .4 percent of the circulation.
- **How much use of the items is done in-house compared to circulation use, if sample is monitored longitudinally?** These records are not available for the Brighton branch.
- **How do the online resources subscribed to by the library supplement this sample collection?** The library system subscribes to 38 databases to supplement the print collection. Anyone with a library card can access the electronic resources remotely. In addition, more than 770 audio books are available for downloading.
- **How does the collection support the library's reference and web site resources, and relate to the social technologies used in the community?** The system has a Twitter account to post news and recently posted a profile on Facebook.

A summary of the collection study follows:

- The collection is current; 80 percent of the titles were added in 2007 or later.

- The collection is heavily used, and usage has recently increased. The average monthly circulation for 2009 (through September) was 24,485, up 21.5 percent from September 2008.
- Adult fiction, children's picture books, and adult nonfiction were the most circulated.
- A system is in place for purchasing multiple copies of a title.
- The monthly average for interlibrary loan orders filled is 109, but that number represents only .4 percent of the total circulation.
- The case study system subscribes to a large number of databases, electronic books, and audio books that supplement the print collection. Anyone with a library card can access the electronic resources remotely.
- The system has a presence on both Facebook and Twitter to reach out to youth and adults who are active in social networking.

A REVIEW OF THE COMMUNITY ANALYSIS PROCESS

As described in Chapter 10, the case study community analysis began with a workshop in August 2008. Data collection teams consisted of a professional working with a paraprofessional at each branch, assisted by a student intern who helped collect and analyze data. Interviews of the project coordinator were conducted monthly. Data collection continued from September through February and included two questionnaires, four community drive-arounds, analysis of phone books and web sites, and a map study. A chronology of the project can be found in Appendix D.

According to the project coordinator, enthusiasm for the project remained high among the branch directors throughout the data collection and analysis period; however, interest lagged among participating paraprofessionals after completion of the map study, the first data collected. Staff were reluctant to distribute the brief questionaires, and the goal of attaining 50 responses from each branch was not reached. Because the surveys were conducted in consecutive two-week periods, staff reported they felt they were harassing customers. Results of the surveys were inconclusive (see Appendix E for a copy of the two surveys administered).

Members of the library district administrative team were apprised of the project's progress at intervals. Results of the data collection were given to the system's Communications Department for synthesis. The final results were used as the basis for a meeting of branch heads when the project was completed.

A study of the data indicated that system-wide, children were served well with collections and services, but the 24–42 age group is not being served. The age distribution is different than previously thought.

In an interview with Lynda Freas (October 21, 2009), the coordinator of the community analysis, she noted that the community analysis results made the librarians more thoughtful of what they were doing; for example, they now pay attention to such statistics as the children's materials circulation, and in comparing it to adult circulation, it indicates a substantial children's audience. Now they analyze data that they did not use before—where resources are circulated and what is circulated. Before the analysis, circulation was the bottom line and the only data monitored. Now they are more intentional about decisions and show interest in more kinds of data. Freas said it is difficult to find the time to do a community analysis, but you can use a great deal of existing data from the integrated library systems for analysis and decision-making.

Authors' Note

The apathy among staff during the case study can be attributed to their lack of involvement. We emphasize the importance of staff participation in the process despite the "busyness" of all staff members. All professionals and paraprofessionals should be involved. A commitment to customer service means a commitment to the **process** of community analysis. During that process, all participants become much more aware of community trends and myths about the library's users and nonusers. The process itself is as informative as the product.

CHAPTER SUMMARY

In this chapter, the community analysis model is applied to a case study library system and library branch. Data were gathered for individuals, groups, agencies, and lifestyles, and from circulation, collection, and registration data. Potential services were extrapolated from the data. This chapter explains what the data mean and how the information gleaned can be used to customize new or existing services in libraries and information agencies. Data collected from the case study will be used to design information services in Chapter 12.

REFERENCES

Bentfield, M. & L. Freas. October 2008. Rangeview Library District. "Where People Come From."

Brighton, Colorado. Greater Brighton Area Chamber of Commerce. http://www.brightonchamber.com/visiting.asp?page=history_tour (accessed November 10, 2009).

Brighton Standard Blade. http://www.thebrightonblade.com/ (accessed November 17, 2009).

City of Brighton. http://www.brightonco.gov/ (accessed November 17, 2009).

DRCOG, Denver Regional Council of Governments. http://www.drcog.org/
    index.cfm (accessed November 17, 2009).
Freas, Lynda. Interviewed October 21, 2009. Mrs. Freas is Director of Family
    Library Services, Anythink, a revolution of Rangeview Libraries, Northglenn,
    Colorado.
Jones, Chandra. Interviewed October 21, 2009. Ms. Jones is Guide, Brighton
    Branch, Anythink, a revolution of Rangeview Libraries, Brighton, Colorado.

CHAPTER 12

Planning Information Services

CHAPTER OVERVIEW

The purpose of conducting a community analysis is to enable the design and implementation of information services that meet the specific needs of customers. By doing this, the library becomes an integral, vital, transformational part of a community. In this chapter we outline a model for planning services and apply that model, using the information collected in our case study.

CONCEPTUALIZING INFORMATION SERVICES

Throughout this book we have emphasized the importance of designing information services based on the identified needs of clientele. The authors have conducted information needs analyses in more than thirty communities for public, school, special, and academic libraries; that work resulted in defining the following categories of information use and corresponding functions of libraries and information agencies:

- Find or locate: The bibliographic (or identification) function of information
- Appreciate: The cultural function of information and books
- Teach or learn: The educational function of information and books
- Create new information or knowledge: The research function
- Decide: The informational function of information
- Enjoy: The recreational function

These categories of information are explained in Greer, Grover, and Fowler (2007), and they are described briefly here. These uses of information lead to the functions of information agencies. For example, people who use information sources to teach or learn are engaged in the educational function. We will discuss each function below.

The reader should be aware that the information professions tend to blend or combine some of the functions in their delivery of services. For example, "reference service" is often the general term used when the service is teaching information skills (educational function), teaching appreciation of good literature (cultural function), providing information for decision making (informational function), assisting the researcher (research function), and helping to locate information (part of the bibliographic function), including the preparation of bibliographies, webographies, pathfinders, and other finding aids. The recreational function too may be considered part of reference services. The authors use the information functions to be more precise in discussing information services.

Functions of Information and Library Services

In this section we provide a brief account of the development of information services by function, along with a description of each function and the various uses of information. We outline implications for the work of information professionals as they design information services (Also see Greer, Grover, and Fowler 2007, 135).

Bibliographic/Archival Function

The archival function (preserving the knowledge of humankind) has been a primary function of libraries for 5,000 years, dating back to ancient cultures, including the Egyptians. Although the format of information storage included clay tablets, papyrus rolls, parchment, velum, palimpsest, and handwritten sheets, the format changed with the invention of the printing press. This fundamental invention enabled mass production of books; however, the archival function remained a primary function of libraries.

Included in this function are the identification, selection, acquisition, organization, storage, retrieval, and preservation of information to provide access to society's records. Because these activities are based primarily on information packages in a variety of printed and electronic formats, they are passive in their level of service (see the definition below in the section "Levels of Service").

The archival function was altered substantially during the eighteenth and nineteenth centuries, when books in libraries were usually listed by title. During these centuries the use of an author's name instead became commonplace. In the nineteenth century, classification schemes were created to facilitate retrieval of books and information by subjects regardless of format. In other words, the bibliographic function expanded the archival function to enable more effective organization, storage, retrieval, and circulation for the use of information, thereby facilitating the other functions noted below.

The focus of the bibliographic function is on what is available and how much can be acquired. The success of this function is measured by the number of items acquired and added to the collection or database and the completeness of the process of acquiring all relevant documents associated with the organization or culture. Since the objective is to maintain an inventory of everything published, this function can be met without a needs assessment of the user population.

The dominant paradigm of librarianship was (and still is, in some libraries) preoccupied with collection development and the acquisition of the best authors in every field, the archival/bibliographic function. In addition, the orderly management of the library staff and facility was paramount. Classification and bibliography were important elements of this paradigm. Missing from the paradigm was service for the library user. There were some papers given at the first American Library Association conference in 1876 that encouraged staff to offer some help to library patrons, but it wasn't until Dewey's staffing of a reference desk that the concept of service was incorporated as a legitimate function of a library. Incidentally, a proper intellectual goal for librarians was to be known as a "bookman" who could identify important works in any field and recite them from memory.

In library and information agencies today, the organization of information for client use is accomplished through bibliographies, indexes, pathfinders, and key word searches and various finding aids, both print and electronic. A systematic or enumerative bibliography is a list of books or other media arranged according to some principle. To implement the bibliographic function effectively, the information professional must know the needs of clientele. Then a finding aid can be developed to address those needs.

While the archival function concentrates on the identification and collection of records as its starting point, this is not true of the educational, recreational, cultural, research, and informational functions. Serving a population with these functions must begin with an assessment of client needs and interests. Once these needs and interests are identified, appropriate resources can be identified, acquired, organized, and delivered by a system specifically designed to reach particular people at particular times and places to satisfy a particular need. Delivery of this customized information may require a system of organization, storage, and retrieval considerably different from that used for the archival function.

Educational Function

The educational function in libraries was introduced with the creation of mercantile and mechanics libraries in major Eastern American cities during the early decades of the nineteenth century. As the industrial revolution developed with the invention of the steam engine, enterprises began to grow in size and complexity. The need for qualified middle level managers required the employment of people outside the limits of the owning families. Therefore, the creation of these libraries was intended to allow young people to educate themselves for industrial careers. A parallel objective was to keep them out of the taverns during their leisure hours.

Another factor in the evolution of public libraries was the movement toward universal public education during the early years of the nineteenth century. Horace Mann and Henry Barnard were leaders of this movement that promoted public libraries as fundamental to the public education of the people. The formal process of initiating the educational function of libraries was inherent in the process DeWitt Clinton, governor of New York, employed in 1835 by encouraging legislation to permit the formation of libraries within the state's school districts. By 1838 no libraries had been organized, and he influenced the adoption of an amendment that provided matching funds from the state for any local effort to create libraries. Perhaps the establishment of these libraries was a matter of convenience so that the library would be placed in a supervised area, the school. Clinton may have thought of these school libraries as public libraries as well.

The 1880s saw the beginning of a paradigm shift in the field of library science. As with many major paradigm shifts, this shift is still in progress today. Two important events occurred during that decade, both initiated by Melvil Dewey, who was director of the libraries of Columbia University in New York City. The first event, in 1887, was initiation of a program of studies at the undergraduate level that Dewey called "library economy." The focus of this program was consistent with the concepts commonly held in the profession, namely that the proper function of the library staff was the orderly management of the library and its collections.

The second event was less striking at the time, but was no less significant than the founding of a program of formal library education. This event was the establishment of formal reference service in the Columbia University Libraries. To implement this service, Dewey employed twin brothers to staff a reference desk full time. The fact that he had committed some of the library's resources for the express purpose of assisting library users in their quest for information was a profound departure from traditional library management. Suddenly, the library user became a meaningful part of the library's purpose. Consequently, what had been a paradigm of book preservation and housekeeping was shattered by the inclusion of users' needs.

Thus, a paradigm shift began in the profession. Large university and municipal libraries soon copied Columbia University's actions.

The educational function of libraries and information agencies supports learning by individuals and groups or classes. This function is one of the oldest forms of service provided by the profession. It is the reason that public libraries were founded in the early 1800s—to serve as a school for the "ordinary person." Schools, especially secondary schools, were out of reach for all but the wealthy. Public libraries were funded in Massachusetts and supported by tax money in order to provide citizens an opportunity to extend their formal schooling.

The educational role of the library has expanded considerably in recent years, and it is still a primary function of most libraries. Clientele visit the library or electronically access the library to learn independently. Librarians and other information professionals have become more engaged in the teaching/learning process. Leading the way have been school and college/university librarians who have collaborated with faculty to teach students information skills. Sometimes called "bibliographic instruction" or "information literacy," information professionals teach people those skills that enable clients to locate, evaluate, and use information effectively.

The educational function engages learners as individuals, in small groups, in formal classes, and in large groups. Learning may occur face-to-face in traditional classrooms or through distant learning in a variety of formats. Libraries in those institutions charged with education have the greatest role in the educational function of information. School library media centers and college and university libraries are highly engaged in fulfilling the educational mission of their parent agencies.

Public libraries are employed in the educational function as well, and complement schools. Some public libraries promote education through collaboration with other agencies, e.g., the local literacy council, adult education program, and book discussion groups, and by providing a high interest/low vocabulary book collection. Public libraries also provide resources to support homeschooling and charter schools.

The school library has an integral role in education. In addition to the prominent role of school library media specialists in student learning, there is a growing function to provide staff development for the school's faculty. Likewise, corporate and other special libraries may play pivotal roles in planning and implementing educational programs for staff and clientele.

Cultural Function

Since their invention, some books have been considered treasures, and the cultural function is a result of that attitude toward books. In the United States, one can picture a handful of classics taken aboard Conestoga wagons as people moved westward, and the cultural function of information was thereby served. The attitude that a book itself was a treasure, a precious object, resulted in books being listed in people's wills. Furthermore, during the expansion of the nation westward in the nineteenth century, new libraries were perceived as the main public cultural resource in the area.

The cultural function of libraries was at the heart of the founding of the American Library Association, which adopted Melvil Dewey's suggested motto: "The best reading for the largest number at the least cost." (Dewey 1978, 77) In his essay on the profession, Dewey (Dewey 1976, 22) wrote: "He [the librarian] must see that his library contains, as far as possible, the best books on the best subjects, regarding carefully the wants of his special community." The term "best reading" reflects the essence of the cultural function of information, i.e., providing clientele the best examples of our cultural heritage as represented in literature, history, music, dance, and various art forms in all formats, digital and analog.

The pervasive value system of library and information agencies currently is to select the "best" available information resources as budgets do not allow for the purchase of every item desired. Consequently, if the acquisition budget is limited (and nearly all but the few libraries in the most affluent communities or corporations have such limitations), the information professional must be selective in choosing the resources for a collection. In a corporate setting, the clientele should be instrumental in determining which are the best journals, databases, books, and other information resources to procure for the collection. Law libraries will collect the electronic and print books and periodicals that are the most reputable and useful in the view of the attorneys and other legal practitioners.

In public and school libraries, the cultural function may be questioned as librarians attempt to lure readers, viewers, and listeners of all ages to use the collection for educational, informational, and recreational purposes. At this point, the term "culture" must be expanded to include the popular literature, music, and art forms of the day. While few will question the inclusion of works by William Shakespeare, Mark Twain, T. S. Eliot, or Robert Browning in a collection because they are recognized as authors of classic literature, should popular authors such as Stephen King (*Carrie*, 1974; *Pet Sematary*, 1983), Dan Brown (*The Da Vinci Code*, 2003) or John Grisham (*The Firm*, 1991; *The King of Torts*, 2004; *Ford County*, 2009; and others) be included in library collections for adults and youth?

The latter examples are popular culture, the literature, music, and art that are popular for a time. One can argue that the popular culture of a generation may endure and become culture in the classic sense. Shakespeare's plays, for example, were very popular with the people of seventeenth century Great Britain. The strength of his characters, his adroit use of language, and strong story lines have endured and will be continue to be studied as part of the English language cultural heritage in future generations.

The cultural function includes the sharing of cultures of various ethnic groups—the music, motion pictures, literature, and customs of immigrants and international cultures. Increasingly we are citizens of a global society, and libraries are repositories for representative artifacts of the cultures of our world.

The cultural function encompasses a variety of formats: books, periodicals, audio recordings in various formats, and video recordings. Consequently, information professionals must be aware of the technologies that record various cultural products and be prepared to select, organize, store, and preserve a variety of formats.

Another reason for including popular culture in library collections is the popular appeal that current authors, artists, and musicians have to attract clientele to use libraries for cultural, educational, or recreational reasons.

Research Function

The research function equates to creating new social knowledge. While we often use the term "research" to indicate that a user of information is "doing library research" to write a paper or report, that context for "research" is really to assist in the educational function, helping a person to learn.

The research function is a by-product of the creation of special libraries. President Abraham Lincoln fostered research contracts with private industry during the Civil War, and researchers needed access to the bodies of their research literature; these collections were the antecedent for special libraries. The Special Libraries Association was formed in 1909 and might be considered the turning point for legitimizing special libraries and the research function that has roots in the movement.

The use of "research" here means that systematic, formal process which requires (1) a review of literature to determine what is state of the art in an area of inquiry, (2) a careful articulation of research questions or hypotheses, (3) a systematic plan and effort to collect data, (4) the analysis of the data, and (5) a report of the results, including generalizations extrapolated from the data. This research is the "scientific" or possibly the "systematic" data-gathering described in Chapter 5. It is the formal, carefully articulated and conducted study that conforms to the scientific paradigm of a discipline or field, or it may be the problem-oriented, practical research conducted by members of a profession. The latter type of research, intended to solve professional problems, is often called "action research." Both types of research contribute new knowledge to a discipline or field of study.

The information professional ideally would be involved at any of the above stages of research: (1) assisting with the key search terms and collaborating with the researcher to conduct a thorough, effective literature review, (2) relating the literature review to the construction of research questions or hypotheses, (3) collaborating with the researcher in planning the research data collection, (4) collaborating in the analysis and interpretation of the data collected, and (5) collaborating on writing the research report. This type of collaboration is currently the standard in many special libraries, especially in the medical and legal fields; it requires the information professional to have the necessary research expertise afforded by an advanced degree in a field, the rationale for university librarians to have a master's degree in library and information science, along with a master's degree in a subject field. Similarly, law librarians may be required to have a Doctor of Juris Prudence (J.D.) degree, or a research library may require a Doctor of Philosophy (Ph.D.) degree.

Engagement in the research process depends on the environment of the information agency. School librarians are rarely engaged in the research function, except in those rare cases when a teacher or principal may request help as they conduct "action research" to solve a professional problem or to fulfill an assignment in a graduate class. However, school librarians and other information professionals may themselves engage in action research to address professional issues, and then publish the results.

In academic libraries, librarians are on-call and can be consulted by faculty to assist with research through in-depth consultation. Information professionals in research libraries and archives often engage with researchers for long periods of time to work on a research project.

Informational Function

Samuel Swett Green and Melvil Dewey first articulated the informational function of libraries when Dewey founded the reference department at Columbia University in the 1880s. Again we point out that the beginning of the paradigm shift from the archival/bibliographic function to the informational function in libraries was a response to library users' needs.

Following World War II, the growth, complexity, range of interests for research contracts, management functions, and the necessity for decision-making required accumulated evidence and experience. Also, professionals who lacked the time and knowledge of information resources to conduct the search for information themselves had a need for access to accumulated research.

Furthermore, the development of computer and telecommunication technology facilitated compilation of database information disconnected from the bibliographic context of its origin. Computerized searching enables the indexing of every word, and information can be retrieved more precisely by words than by subject headings or concepts.

The informational function provides information for decision making. Providing information to people instead of teaching them how to use information sources is not a new concept in the library and information profession; however, the implementation of information service has been slow to evolve. Samuel S. Green was one of the first librarians to write about information service. He emphasized the importance of working with people to meet their needs: "A librarian should be as unwilling to allow an inquirer to leave the library with his question unanswered as a shopkeeper is to have a customer go out of his store without making a purchase" (Green 1976, 327).

The Reference and User Services Association (RUSA), a division of the American Library Association, articulates the following goal in its "Guidelines for Information Service:"

> The goal of information services is to provide the information sought by the user. Information service should anticipate as well as meet user needs. It should encourage user awareness of the potential of information resources to fulfill individual information needs. (Reference and User Services Association, 2000)

The informational function is usually called "reference service" or "information service" in today's libraries and information centers. As noted above, the reference or information function of the library was formally introduced by Melvil Dewey at the Columbia University library in the 1880s. By creating a reference department and assigning staff to this function, Dewey deliberately designated some of his resources specifically for the benefit of the clientele rather than for housekeeping the collection.

Reference service is found in nearly all libraries. This service includes the teaching of information skills (really the educational function), ready reference, and regular reference service. "Ready reference" is the term used for questions that can be answered very quickly by consulting one or two information sources. Bopp and Smith (2001, 7) give these examples of ready reference questions:

- An address
- The spelling or definition of a word
- A date or place of an event
- Something about the life or career of an individual
- Bibliographic verification, which provides accurate information about published and mass distributed information sources in all formats—authors, publishers/producers, date of release, etc.
- Interlibrary loan and document delivery, a service which identifies locations of resources in other libraries and provides for the delivery of these information items to a client
- Information and referral services, which identify community agencies and individuals who can supply wanted information

In most information agencies, some type of information service is provided, sometimes for a fee. If a service requires an extraordinary amount of a professional's time, the client may be charged, especially in special libraries. Even some public libraries have charged fees for their services when that service was beyond the standard service for clientele.

In corporate, government, legal, medical, and other libraries and information centers, the provision of direct information may include reports as part of the service to clientele. For example, an information professional may be asked to conduct a search of all of the laws adopted during the last ten years in a state and synthesize a brief report of each law's content. The synthesizing and summarizing of complex information is an important skill that is especially valuable for managers and executives in all types of agencies. Professionals with the ability to locate and summarize information quickly, concisely, and accurately are highly valuable to an organization. As the amount of information available becomes greater, these skills are in demand even more.

Recreational Function

The recreational function is associated with the advent of the paperback book in the 1930s and 1940s. This new format transformed the book from a treasure to a disposable commodity. This use of books and other forms of information has assumed greater importance in public libraries as technology has produced entertainment packages in the format of compact disks, computer software (games), and DVDs. School, most special, and college/university libraries tend to de-emphasize the recreational function, citing budget constraints; resources are instead devoted to the archival/ bibliographic, educational, cultural, research, or informational function that addresses the mission of that agency and library.

The recreational function is synonymous with enjoyment. It is concerned with the use of information resources during leisure time. These resources include novels, poetry, periodicals, nonfiction, audio recordings, video recordings, and games to support leisure time interests.

The recreational use of libraries might be controversial for some members of the public and for some information professionals. The recreational function was not one of the original functions of libraries. It was not mentioned prominently in the literature of the profession until the latter part of the twentieth century. The inclusion of paperback books as acceptable items for library collections generally was not embraced until after World War II. The expendable nature of the paperback format violated the social norm that books were treasures to be valued as artifacts.

The rationale often given is that the recreational function of a library is a way of reaching people who may not otherwise use the library, or who cannot afford to buy the resources, or simply don't want to pay for them if they are "only" recreational. Once in the library, staff may steer clientele to other resources and services that will benefit the individual. We believe that the reason to include recreational resources is to meet the recreational needs and wants of clientele, and that recreational needs are as important to quality of life as educational or cultural or informational needs. Another point is that today's recreational materials just may be tomorrow's classics.

Information and Library Services Functions Summary

Information services typically cross the functions categories, but they were launched to meet specific needs of individuals. Not included were such services as conducting online searches with or without the consultation with a user. As technology becomes more sophisticated, especially with the integration of "smart" computers (or artificial intelligence), the ability for computers to diagnose the information needs of clientele will be a major contributor to the advancement of information services in the future.

As technology becomes "smarter," and as our world changes, library and information professionals must be mindful of other information services that should be offered to meet different and evolving information needs. Similarly, traditional services may have to be discontinued. To make these decisions, professionals must continuously monitor the changing environment and changing society. We cannot be complacent with successful services offered; in fact, success often breeds satisfaction and ennui, stifling innovation. More on this topic is found in Chapter 13.

Levels of Service

A model for outlining levels of service was introduced by Greer and Hale (1982) and updated by Greer, Grover, and Fowler (2007). This model uses the terms "passive," "reactive," and "assertive" service.

Passive Service

"The passive level of service consists of a process of choosing, acquiring, and organizing materials on the library shelves for the user to discover." (Greer, Grover, and Fowler 2007, 142) In a passive service the information professional does not engage with the client to assist with the understanding or use of the information. In a passive library or information center, the information agency provides access to a collection of books, journals, databases, or other media for use by clientele with no assistance from staff.

Reactive Service

Reactive service provides information on request by the clientele. An example is the traditional reference service provided in most libraries, when information is provided upon customer request. Another example is the provision of finding aids (bibliographies. mediagraphies, or webographies) upon request. The resource collection and programs offered are based on the librarian's professional judgment of relevance to the community. Input from the community is welcomed, but there is no systematic effort to assess the information needs of that community.

Assertive Service

This level of service addresses the known information needs of clientele as identified by an information needs analysis. This level of service anticipates information need, and information is delivered to clientele without their asking. For example, a university librarian may e-mail a faculty member a newly arrived journal article for a literature review the professor is preparing. Or, a school library media specialist, knowing the calendar of subjects to be taught to seventh grade history students, arranges a meeting with history teachers to plan a history unit which integrates the teaching of notetaking skills.

The keys to an assertive level of service are (1) the systematic collection of community data from which needs and interests are inferred, (2) the development of a customized collection, and (3) the dissemination of information to meet both the inferred and expressed needs. The central focus of this level of service is the community and its people (Greer, Grover, and Fowler 2007, 142–143).

These levels of service can be applied to the various information functions or services described earlier in this chapter. Those services can be provided at different levels, as depicted in Table 12.1 below.

The matrix above is a model for considering the variety of services that can be offered in a library or information agency. The analysis of need and development of services in response are the essence of the library and information professions.

Table 12.1   **Information Functions and Levels of Service.**

	Passive	Reactive	Assertive
Bibliographic/Archival			
Cultural			
Educational			
Research			
Informational			
Recreational			

PUTTING IT ALL TOGETHER: THE ROLE
OF THE PROFESSIONAL

Butler's (1933, 105–106) philosophy describes well the role of the information professional:

> The library is no mission station for the promulgation of an established literary gospel that is eternally true. The librarian's duty is not to entice men, against their wills if it need be, to convert themselves to his way of thinking. He is merely society's custodian of its cultural archives. The responsibility which he assumes with his office is to exploit those archives for communal advantage to the utmost extent of his ability. Therefore, a major phase of the library's service to any individual reader will be to assist him to an effective method for achieving his own private purpose, so long as this is not anti-social, and to safeguard him from listing his labor in activities which are futile with reference to his own immediate desire. For all this, there must be a sympathetic understanding of the individual's motive and mental ability. Effective librarianship is largely a matter of accurate psychological diagnosis.

Butler's comments about libraries and books is generalizable across various types of information agencies: libraries, archives, information centers, private enterprise, and government agencies. All information service begins with knowledge of the clientele, their roles, and the information needed for those roles. When information needs have been identified, information services can be planned to address those needs at three levels: passive, reactive, and assertive. The services can be classified into six categories of information function: educational, cultural, research, recreational, informational, and bibliographic. It is this process of diagnosing information needs, planning and implementing services, and evaluating the impact of services that comprises the essential role of the library and information professional.

Applying Data to Service Scenarios

At this point we have data about our case study community, and we have a model for thinking about types and levels of information services. Now we are ready to merge this knowledge into a plan for possible services in our case study community.

As a review, we earlier studied census data on **individuals** in Brighton and offered these generalizations:

- The age groups are evenly distributed, with no dominant age group, suggesting a wide range of services for people of all ages.

- The community is well educated. Nearly half of the population has more than a high school education; 17.6 percent have a bachelor's or master's degree.
- There is a substantial Hispanic population (39.1%) that could be a target audience for services.

Studying the types and numbers of **groups** suggests the following generalizations:

- There are several groups of young mothers who could benefit from programs and resources devoted to parenting young children.
- Because scout leaders are volunteers, the scouting group leaders (and leaders of all groups) need information pertaining to leadership and running meetings.
- Scout leaders could use information about the psychological and physical development of children.
- The seniors in the community may be interested in resources on the aging process, good health habits, diet, travel, hobbies, and money management.
- The various health groups could use resources related to their interests—recovery from alcoholism, drug dependency, obesity, etc.
- The various cultural groups suggest a need for a good collection of resources on the arts.

The analysis of **agencies** revealed possible opportunities for library collaboration include:

- Working with Youth Services to bring educational, cultural, and recreational resources to area youth
- Partnering with churches to offer such services as English language training and enculturation of Hispanic population into the Brighton community
- Providing cultural services through the educational agencies, especially the art academy, studios, and theatre company
- Collaborating with the chamber of commerce to provide business information to startup companies as well as smaller companies that lack information professionals and information resources

The study of **lifestyles** resulted in the following generalizations that have implications for information services:

- The city has grown and will continue to grow—the population more than doubled from 1980 to 2005 and is expected to nearly double again by 2030, an increase of 88 percent.

- Only one-third of the Brighton workforce population works in Brighton. Workers commute to their jobs and are probably willing to drive moderate distances for library and information services, and audio tapes could be used during commutes between home and work.
- The residents are multi-ethnic, with about 38 percent being of Hispanic descent, and 11 percent of the population speaking little English, again suggesting a need for cultural and educational services.
- Nearly 40 percent of the Brighton population are younger adults (ages 20–44) of child-rearing age

If we apply these generalizations, we might develop services using the functions matrix, and it could look like Table 12.2 below. This chart is an example and is not intended to be a comprehensive plan for library services.

We hasten to add that all of these services may not be possible because of staff and budget constraints. For example, some services offered are dependent upon the strengths of the library professional staff; those with a history

Table 12.2 Possible Information Services for Brighton.

Service	Passive	Reactive	Assertive
Bibliographic/ Archival	• Provide a current catalog of resources	• Help clients locate information when asked	• Based on need, develop bibliographies, web sites, pathfinders, and other finding aids
Cultural	• Establish a Spanish collection of resources • Develop collections on the arts • Consult with school librarians for resources to support the curriculum • Need resources to teach English language and American culture	• Staff are prepared to answer questions related to culture • Requests should be recorded and mediagraphies & pathfinders developed according to interests	• Offer cultural programs in collaboration with the art academy, studios, and theatre company • Offer English as a 2nd language (ESL) classes

(*continued*)

Service	Passive	Reactive	Assertive
Educational	• Provide resources for parenting • Collect resources on leadership and meeting management • Develop collection on child development • For seniors collect resources on the aging process, good health habits, diet, and money management • Resources are needed for drug and alcohol recovery	• Same as above services	• Offer ongoing classes on parenting • For seniors, offer programs on aging, health, & money management • Offer drug & alcohol recovery program in collaboration with health agencies
Research	• Collection should include basic sources on research methods	• Assist with searches on request • Refer research questions to faculty in higher education institutions	• None
Informational	• Build business collection, including business databases	• Provide a fast-response information service for businesses using e-mail and telephone • Provide general reference service by phone, in person, and by e-mail	• Collaborate with the chamber of commerce to provide business information to startup and smaller companies
Recreational	• Book and nonprint collection should provide for a wide range of reading ability and interests. Need resources on travel and hobbies, especially for seniors. • Build collection of audio books for commuters	• Provide for client input in the selection of recreational resources in various formats.	• Collaborate with the city's recreation department to offer recreational activities

degree will be able to answer cultural questions accurately and comprehensively, but there may be no one on the staff who can speak Spanish in order to answer the cultural questions of those clients who speak little or no English. Planning should take advantage of the academic strengths, hobbies, and interests of the staff, including paraprofessionals as well as professionals.

After a community analysis has outlined possible services as in the chart above, a meeting or several meetings should be held to enable staff-wide input for prioritizing services—some services can and should be offered immediately, while others must be postponed because of budget constraints or a requirement for staff training. At the same time, staff should use data from the community analysis to decide which current services are **not** needed and can be discontinued to free up resources for addressing current needs.

The most important concept here is that the decisions should all be based on data collected from the community. While staff impressions and intuition will be voiced, the data from the community add plausibility to the more informal data collection based on experience in the library. In other words, decisions should no longer be made by "the seat of your pants."

SUMMARY

Today's society requires a high level of service in order for libraries and information agencies to be successful within their communities. The definition of **community** varies by type of information agency. Private enterprise, schools, special libraries, and even colleges and universities have communities that are rather easily identified and have defined missions. Public libraries, on the other hand, are highly complex, and we have used public libraries for our case study and our examples and discussion. We want to emphasize that while the definition of a community varies by type of information agency, the philosophy and techniques presented here can be adapted for any type of information agency.

A key to success in an information agency is the staff's ability to assess information needs, design information services to meet those needs, implement the services, and evaluate the service to fine tune it. The diagnostic interview and community analysis are essential tools which enable information professionals to customize services transform individuals, groups, and potentially, communities. The design of services can be the outcome of a community analysis, and attributing levels of service (passive, reactive, assertive) is a way of conceptualizing options for administering a needed service, depending on needs and the library resources available to address those information needs.

Any type of information agency can apply the functions matrix in planning services. Conceptualizing services by function (educational, informational, cultural, research, recreational, or bibliographic), the information professional can apply this model to the design of information services for an identified population.

REFERENCES

Bopp, Richard E. and Linda K. Smith. 2001. *Reference and information services: An introduction.* Englewood, CO: Libraries Unlimited.

Brown, Dan. 2003. *The Da Vinci Code.* Sumas, WA: Discover Books.

Butler, Pierce. 1933. *An Introduction to Library Science.* Chicago: The University of Chicago Press.

Dewey, Melvil. 1978. "Origin of the A. L. A. motto." In *Melvil Dewey: His enduring presence in librarianship,* ed. Sarah K.Vann, 77. Littleton, CO: Libraries Unlimited.

Dewey, Melvil. 1976. "The profession." In *Landmarks of Library Literature, 1876–1976,* ed. Dianne J. Ellsworth and Norman D. Stevens, 21–23. Metuchen, NJ: The Scarecrow Press.

Green, Samuel S. 1976. "Personal relations between librarians and readers." In *Landmarks of Library Literature, 1876–1976,* ed. Dianne J. Ellsworth and Norman D. Stevens, 319–330. Metuchen, NJ: The Scarecrow Press.

Greer. Roger C., Robert J. Grover, and Susan G. Fowler. 2007. *Introduction to the library and information professions.* Westport, CT and London: Libraries Unlimited.

Greer, Roger C. and Martha L. Hale. 1982. "The community analysis process." In *Public librarianship, a reader,* ed. Jane Robbins-Carter, 358–366. Littleton, CO: Libraries Unlimited.

Grisham, John. 1991. *The Firm.* New York: Random House.

———. 2004. *The King of Torts.* New York: Random House.

———. 2009. *Ford County.* New York: Random House.

King, Stephen. 1974. *Carrie.* New York: Doubleday.

———. 1983. *Pet Sematary.* New York: Doubleday.

Reference and User Services Association. 2000. Guidelines for information services http://www.ala.org/ala/mgrps/divs/rusa/resources/guidelines/ guidelinesinformation.cfm (accessed December 10, 2009).

CHAPTER 13

Issues in Implementation

CHAPTER OVERVIEW

Community analysis requires a customer-centered philosophy and a commitment to addressing the changing needs of clientele. Information professionals are busy people, yet knowing customers is a prerequisite to providing leadership in a responsive, vital organization that meets the needs of its community.

This chapter looks to leading thinkers in the business world to define a rationale for customer-centered services, emphasizing the need for continuous monitoring of societal and community trends in order to remain a viable organization supported by the community it serves. Providing customized services and products that exceed customer expectations is the key to success for any service agency. Examples are given from successful businesses, and implications are specified for libraries and information agencies.

TODAY'S BUSINESS ENVIRONMENT

The twenty-first century is still young, but already it has spawned a number of daunting challenges. As the pace of change accelerates, many companies are on the wrong side of the change curve. Entire industries have been overtaken by change, e.g., traditional airlines, old-line department stores, network television, American auto makers, and newspapers.

Digitization has threatened the companies that create and sell intellectual property, e.g., movie makers, drug companies, and book publishers. The Internet is shifting bargaining power from the producer to the consumer. The life cycle of a business has been shortened by such factors as outsourcing and the Internet. "Today the parabola of success is often a short, sharp spike" (Hamel and Breen 2007, 10).

All of these changes also influence libraries and information agencies of all types. What worked in the past may not work in the future. Even the way we measure success in libraries must change. Counting books, the size of the resource collection, the budget, number of staff, and even circulation are not accurate measures of a library's impact. Instead, we must look at output, the impact of libraries on their constituent organizations and customers. James LaRue, Director of Douglas County Colorado Libraries, has this to say about measuring the effectiveness of public libraries:

> The next frontier of performance measurement won't be just about how well the library does library stuff. It will be about demonstrating the impact of good libraries on the towns, cities, and counties in which they operate. (2009)

The same holds true for all types of information agencies. They must continuously monitor their outputs and their impact lest they fail like some companies in the private sector.

A recent study by the OCLC, from awareness to funding, showed that supporters of public libraries, those most likely to vote for funding increases, see the library as a community resource just like schools, fire departments, and police. These strong supporters are willing to increase their taxes to support the library, and they perceive the library as more than a provider of information through its collections; these committed supporters believe that the library is a transformational force in the community (De Rosa and Johnson 2008, 5, 7–4). We contend that all information agencies should heed the results of this research. When libraries are **transformational** in the lives of individuals and in their communities, they are integral services that will be sustained by their communities. To do this, libraries must be willing to change with their communities.

Large companies have become dinosaurs because they were overtaken by change, e.g., Kodak, Sony, Sears, General Motors, Toys R Us, and Sun Microsystems. They failed to reinvent themselves in a timely fashion (Hamel and Breen 2007, 42). A troubling trend for organizations—businesses and other organizations such as libraries—is that few can manage deep and meaningful change:

> A review of the extensive library on managing change reveals a disturbing fact. Nearly all the accounts of deep change—entailing big shifts in a company's business model or core mission—are stories of turnarounds, with a new CEO typically cast as the hero. It seems that deep change is nearly always crisis-led, episodic, and programmatic—accomplished

through a top-to-bottom cascade of tightly scripted messages, events, goals, and actions. Sadly, it is rarely opportunity-led, continuous, and a product of the organization's intrinsic capacity to learn and adapt. (Hamel and Breen 2007, 43)

Leading Change

Who in an organization is responsible for that organization's adapting to a changing environment? It is the leadership, the professionals in an organization, and we look to Peter Drucker, a long-time intellectual leader in business, to provide his rationale for leading change. He outlined three tasks that face the management of an organization:

- To define the purpose and mission of the institution
- To make the work productive and the worker achieving
- To manage social impact (Drucker 2008, 26)

Professionals in libraries and other information agencies are charged with this leadership as well. To accomplish these tasks, Drucker declared that an organization must have a

"theory of business," which has three parts: (1) assumptions about the environment of the organization, i.e., society, the market or audience, the customer, and technology; (2) assumptions about the mission of the organization; and (3) assumptions about the core competencies needed to accomplish the organization's mission. (Drucker 2008, 89)

Successfully defining and implementing a theory of business requires, among other things, that the assumptions about mission, environment, and core competencies be consistent with reality, and that the theory of business must be tested constantly because society, markets, customers, and technology are in constant flux. An organization must continuously monitor its environment in order to keep pace with change. Community analysis provides the methodology for monitoring change.

Furthermore, Drucker emphasized the importance of an enterprise knowing its customers in order to state its mission. The first question to address is: What is our business?

With respect to the definition of business purpose and business mission, there is only one such focus, one starting point. It is the customer. The customer defines the business. A business is not defined by the company's name, statutes, or articles of incorporation. It is defined by the want the customer satisfies when he or she buys a product or a service. To satisfy the customer is the mission and purpose of every business. The question, What is our business? can, therefore, be answered only by looking at the business from the outside, from the point of view of customer and market. (Drucker 2001, 24)

Implementing a System for Change

Because of the rapid pace of societal change, organizations must be wary of their business theory becoming obsolete. To guard against obsolescence, there must be preventive care to bring the organization's behavior in line with its environment. Drucker (2008) recommends two such preventive measures: abandonment and studying noncustomers (Drucker 2008, 91–93).

To address the preventive measure of abandonment, every organization should challenge all products, services, polices, and distribution channels every three years. This question should be asked: "If we were not in it already, would we be going into it now?" (Drucker 2008, 91) The purpose of this is to test accepted policies and procedures and to test their assumptions. Why are some practices working? Why are other practices not working? If an organization does not engage in systematic abandonment of practices that do not work, it will lack the resources to take advantage of new opportunities when there is change in markets, technologies, and core competencies.

The second preventive measure, studying noncustomers, helps an organization to identify trends which do not occur inside the organization or within its customer base. Change usually occurs with noncustomers, who nearly always outnumber customers. For example, Wal-Mart claims 20 percent of the U.S. consumer goods market, meaning that 80 percent of the retail market is noncustomers to them.

An example of studying noncustomers applies to department stores. Thirty years ago department stores were at their peak, serving 30 percent of the non-food retail market. They carefully studied their customers, but they ignored noncustomers. Their theory of business was that people who could afford department stores did their shopping there. That theory fit the market sixty years ago, but when baby boomers became adults, the theory was no longer valid. The dominant shopping group among baby boomers was women in educated two-income families. For these women, money did not determine where they would shop; time was the important factor. These career women did not have the time to shop in department stores; they were looking for convenience (Drucker 2008, 92–93).

Service organizations whose service was taken for granted are now under fire for lack of performance. Colleges, hospital, and universities have grown remarkably, but they are in crisis. Are libraries? When the public criticizes agencies for their bureaucracy, "[w]hat they mean is that the government agency is being run more for the convenience of its employees than for *contribution* and *performance*" (Drucker 2008, 132).

To survive and thrive in a fast-paced society, all service institutions must impose on themselves the following kinds of discipline:

1. Define their business and what it should be—a mission.
2. Derive clear goals and objectives from the mission.
3. Set priorities to enable the setting of standards for mission accomplishment and performance.
4. Define performance measures—as determined by customers.
5. Use these measures to review efforts.
6. Systematically review the objectives and results to eliminate those objectives that no longer are workable.

Drucker provides a sound rationale for these measures:

Without a market test, the service institution lacks the built-in discipline that forces a business eventually to abandon yesterday—or else go bankrupt. Assessing and abandoning low-performance activities in service institutions, outside and inside business, would be the most painful but also the most beneficial improvement. (Drucker 2008, 133)

Market testing is especially difficult for public service agencies like libraries, who must fight for their budgets and provide services with limited staff; however, monitoring the market must assures efficiency and organization viability.

This corporate willingness to monitor activities continuously is referred to by Weick and Sutcliffe (2007) as "mindful management." Through their study of high reliability organizations (HROs), Weick and Sutcliffe observed that organizations that coped effectively with uncertainty and successfully managed unexpected events acted mindfully. They were organized in such a way that they were better able to notice the unexpected and halt its development. By "mindful" Weick and Sutcliffe also mean that an organization " … is distinguished by continuous updating and deepening of increasingly plausible interpretations of the context, what problems define it, and what remedies it contains" (Weick and Sutcliffe 2008, 18). In other words, organizations must carefully and continuously monitor their environment and their communities.

It is most difficult for an institution to abandon an activity that was, at one time, successful. Indeed, success can impede change, and an organization must have a system that supports both change and mindful management.

The importance of data-driven change is reinforced by Collins's research of great companies. Summarizing the characteristics of companies that have grown to become successful, Collins wrote that one of the dominant themes from his research is that results come about by a series of good decisions, well executed and accumulated one on top of another. Furthermore, these decisions were led by an ambitious, humble leader with capable team members, and driven by "brutal facts" carefully and systematically gathered (Collins 2001, 69).

RETAINING CUSTOMERS

Ultimately, information agencies and businesses want to satisfy their customers and retain them. *Harvard Business Review* studies have shown that customer satisfaction is not enough to keep customers; an enterprise must *delight* customers. "Studies conducted by HBR revealed that 65–85 percent of customers who chose a new supplier said they were satisfied or very satisfied with their former supplier. It is hard enough to meet a customer's expectations, let alone exceed them, if a firm does not know exactly what they are" (Dunn and Baker 2003, 118).

Because customer expectations are dynamic, not static, an enterprise must continuously ask customers what they expect at least annually (Dunn and Baker 2003, 118). Dunn and Baker cite a Rockefeller Corporation study of why customers leave a company:

- 1%: The customer dies.
- 3%: The customer moves away.
- 5%: The customer has a friend who provides the service.
- 9%: The customer is lost to a competitor.
- 14%: The customer is dissatisfied with some aspect of the service.
- 68%: The customer believes you don't care about them.

In summary, in seven of ten cases, people leave a company because they don't believe you care (Dunn and Baker 2003, 140)! If information agencies want repeat business, they must also provide a caring environment for their clientele.

THE CHALLENGE AHEAD

The underlying philosophy of this book has been this: Know your community and your clientele. Libraries and other information agencies are supported by their communities, whether they are municipalities, higher education institutions, school districts, private enterprises, or public agencies (hospitals, government, etc.). Every type of organization must continuously demonstrate its contribution to the greater community and to be an integral part of that community. To serve that community and become transformational elements in that community, leaders must be aware of that community and its constituents' changing information needs. Failure to identify these needs and to develop and implement assertive information services to address those needs will eventually result in failure and eventual budget cuts. Indeed, libraries could go the way of General Motors—failure to keep up with change can mean bankruptcy or closure.

We suggest thinking of libraries and information agencies as businesses that are determined to know their customers and to serve them well—to the extent that the library becomes integral to the mission of the organization and acts as a transformational agent in the organization. As research has demonstrated, customers return when their expectations have been **exceeded**. Therefore, information services should not only be reactive to needs, they must **anticipate** needs and provide services that address those needs. In other words, aim to provide services that clientele aren't even aware that they need.

Using Jim Collins's research as a guideline, our philosophy as library and information professionals should be to make our libraries more than good— they should be made GREAT! We can do that only when we understand our customers' needs and translate those needs into transformational services.

REFERENCES

Collins, Jim. 2001. *Good to Great: Why Some Companies Make the Leap . . . And Others Don't*. New York: HarperBusiness.

De Rosa, Cathy and Jenny Johnson. 2008. *From awareness to funding: A study of library support in America. A report to the OCLC membership*. Principal contributors Cathy De Rosa and Jenny Johnson. Dublin, OH: OCLC. http:// www.oclc.org/reports/funding/default.htm (accessed December 10, 2009).

Drucker, Peter F. 1995. *Managing in a Time of Great Change*. New York: Truman Talley Books/Dutton.

———. 2001. *The Essential Drucker*. New York: HarperBusiness.

———. 2008. *Management*. Revised edition. With Joseph A. Maciariello. New York: Collins.

Dunn, Paul and Ronald J. Baker. 2003. *The Firm of the Future: A Guide for Accountants, Lawyers, and Other Professional Services*. Hoboken, NJ: John Wiley & Sons.

Hamel, Gary and Bill Breen. 2007. *The Future of Management*. Boston, MA: Harvard Business School Press.

LaRue, James. Libraries should measure community impact. September 3, 2009. http://www.douglascountylibraries.org/AboutUs/LaRuesViews/2009/ 090309 (accessed March 1, 2010).

Weick, Karl E. and Kathleen M. Sutcliffe. *Managing the unexpected; resilient performance in an age of uncertainty*. 2007. 2nd edition. San Francisco: Jossey-Bass.

APPENDIX A: EDUCATIONAL ATTAINMENT FOR THE SIX COMMUNITIES

Community	Less Than 9th Grade	9–12 grade, no diploma	High School Grade	Some College	Associate's Degree	Bachelor's Degree	Graduate or Professional Degree
Bennett	3.5%	8.9%	36.9%	30.6%	7.9%	10.5%	1.8%
Brighton	6.4%	11.8%	33.3%	23.8%	7.1%	11.6%	6.0%
Commerce City	11.1%	19.1%	30.8%	18.8%	4.1%	12.5%	3.6%
Northglenn	6.9%	9.9%	33.1%	24.2%	8.0%	13.7%	4.2%
Perl Mack	13.5%	16.9%	33.7%	20.7%	5.3%	7.0%	3.0%
Thornton	4.5%	9.2%	30.5%	22.8%	8.5%	17.7%	6.8%
Community Mean	7.7%	12.6%	33.1%	23.5%	6.8%	12.2%	4.2%

APPENDIX B: BRIGHTON BUSINESSES BY CATEGORY

Business Category	Number	Business Category	Number
Accounting firms	5	Health care	8
Advertising/marketing	7	Home improvement	4
Apartment complexes	3	Horseback riding/stable	1
Assisted living	1	Insurance agencies	19
Attorneys' offices	5	Investment brokers	5
Automobile dealers	4	Landscaping	4
Auto/trucks parts & repairs	5	Liquor stores	1
Banks	9	Manufacturing	3
Beauty shops	5	Meal preparation	1
Business assistance/consulting	5	Military recruiting	1
Car/truck rental	2	Monuments	1
Catering services	2	Mortgage services	5
Computer servicing	1	Motels/lodging	3
Construction	4	Movie theaters	0
Employment services	1	Newspapers	2
Engineering firm	1	Real estate agencies	14
Farm supplies	2	Real estate developers	4
Financial services	2	Restaurants	2
Flooring	1	Retail stores	5
Florists	2	Tax services	2
Funeral homes	0	Transportation (public)	2
Golf course	1	Veterinarians	3
Gyms/fitness centers	1	Web design & hosting	0
Hardware	1		

APPENDIX C: BRIGHTON'S HISTORY

Brighton has a long history in agriculture and business and was established as the commerce center of the area when it became a stop along the Front Range rail line in 1884. The first official "industry" in the town was the Brighton Creamery—also established in 1884—where local farmers went to sell their milk. Brighton-area produce has been a key product in the state of Colorado, dating back to 1889, when the Brighton Canning Company began. However, that company failed after a few years, as did the Colorado Vinegar and Pickle Company, which followed soon after. But in 1907, Max Kuner, who owned a large canning company in Greeley, built a small facility in Brighton to package sauerkraut and pickles. This venture worked and the Kuner facility was later sold to Stokely-Van Camp, and continues to provide a market for local farmers today. Railroad construction in the area attracted a large number of Japanese laborers, many who would eventually settle in the Brighton area. By the early 1900s several Japanese-American groups had formed, eventually leading to the current Brighton Japanese American Association. The group, representing citizens of varied backgrounds, is a strong and vital force in the town.

In the early part of the century, Colorado "wheelmen" (now known as "bicyclists") considered Brighton the local center of their sport. In fact, the Brighton Wheel Club sponsored a number of challenging road races, and remained active until the popularity of the car overwhelmed the club. It was this early commitment to cycling that was key to helping Adams County build an interlocking system of hiking and biking trails throughout the county. Throughout the last century (until the 1970s), the Brighton Sugar Factory was vital to the city. In the early 1900s Brighton processed thousands of pounds of sugar beets into sugar. At its height, the plant processed six hundred tons of beets every day and was the most important industry in the area. Farmers were paid according to the sugar content of the beets they delivered. The industry prospered for years, until the Great Western Sugar Company closed the facility in 1977.

Today, Brighton's economy is as diverse as it ever has been. Some of the companies that keep our residents working include: American Pride Coop, Interstate Polymer Group, Kmart Distribution Center, Platte Valley Medical Center, United Power, Wayne's Electric, and Western United Electric Supply Corporation (Brighton Chamber of Commerce web site).

APPENDIX D: CASE STUDY CHRONOLOGY

August   Workshop for branch directors, selected staff, administrators

September   Branches conduct a map study of users' home locations

                 Intern begins analysis of census data

October   Intern continues analysis of census data

                 First customer survey is distributed to branches for 2 weeks

                 Map study results are displayed at the library board meeting

November   Second customer survey is distributed to branches for 2 weeks

                 Decreasing interest of staff becomes apparent

December   Branch representatives are asked to list community contacts on childcare, social organizations, help organizations, schools, local businesses, different agencies, churches, etc. They are to use newspapers, phone books, any sources that will help.

January   Community data have been collected

                 Drive-arounds are done in 4 communities

February   Preliminary results are presented to the administrative executive team

                 Data analysis by intern continues

March   Data analysis by intern continues

April   Communication Department begins assembling snapshots of
                 branch demographics

May   Completed branch snapshots are presented to branch heads
                 for discussion of implications

APPENDIX E: CASE STUDY SURVEY QUESTIONS

Case Study Survey #1
Rangeview: Getting to know our community

◇ What are your hobbies?

♣ Do you play sports? If so, what are they?

♡ What outdoor activities do you enjoy?

♠ What do you do during your leisure time?

If you could get more information on any of these activities, what format would you prefer? (Books, DVD, audio book, e-book, CD, etc).

Case Study Survey #2
Rangeview: Getting to know our community

◇ What type of computer games do you enjoy?

♣ What type of board games do you enjoy?

♡ What types of clubs or teams are you a part of?

♠ Are you a member of any organizations?

❖ Do you attend any meetings that play a significant role in your life?

SELECTED BIBLIOGRAPHY

We list here works consulted and thought to be of value to readers continuing their study of issues related to community analysis.

Adams, Mignon S. and Jeffrey A. Beck. 1995. *User surveys in college libraries*. CLIP Note #23. Chicago: Association of College and Research Libraries, a Division of the American Library Association.

Aguilar, Francis Joseph. 1967. *Scanning the Business Environment*. New York and London: Macmillan.

Armour, Richard Willard. 1976. *The Happy Bookers: A Playful History of Librarians and Their World from the Stone Age to the Distant Future*. New York: McGraw-Hill.

Battles, Matthew. 2003. *Library: An Unquiet History*. New York: W.W. Norton.

Bopp, Richard E. and Linda K. Smith. 2001. *Reference and information services: An introduction*. Englewood, CO: Libraries Unlimited.

Bourgeois, L. J. III, "Strategy making, environment, and economic performance: a conceptual and empirical exploration." Doctoral dissertation, University Microfilms International in Costa, Jorge. 1995. An empirically-based review of the concept of environmental scanning. *International Journal of Contemporary Hospitality Management*, 7, 7, 4–9.

Butler, Pierce. 1933. *An Introduction to Library Science*. Chicago: The University of Chicago Press.

Carnovsky, Leon. 1934. A study of the relationship between reading interest and actual reading. *Library Quarterly*, 4, 1, 76–110.

Casson, Lionel. 2001. *Libraries in the Ancient World*. New Haven: Yale University Press.

Cleveland, Harlan. 1985. *The Knowledge Executive: Leadership in an Information Society*. New York: Truman Talley Books/E. P. Dutton.

Collins, Jim. 2001. *Good to Great: Why Some Companies Make the Leap ... And Others Don't.* New York: HarperBusiness.

Costa, Jorge. 1995. An empirically-based review of the concept of environmental scanning. *International Journal of Contemporary Hospitality Management,* 7, 7, 4–9.

D'Elia, George and Eleanor Jo Rodger. 1991. *Free Library of Philadelphia patron survey: Final report.* University of Minnesota Center for Survey Research.

———. 1994. Public library roles and patron use: why patrons use the library. *Public Libraries, 33,* 135–44.

———. 1996. Customer satisfaction with public libraries. *Public Libraries, 35,* 292–7.

De Rosa, Cathy and Jenny Johnson. 2008. *From awareness to funding: A study of library support in America: A report to the OCLC membership.* Principal contributors Cathy De Rosa and Jenny Johnson. Dublin, OH: OCLC. http://www.oclc.org/reports/funding/default.htm (accessed December 10, 2009).

Dewey, Melvil. 1978. Origin of the A. L. A. motto. In *Melvil Dewey: His Enduring Presence in Librarianship,* ed. Sarah K.Vann, 77. Littleton, CO: Libraries Unlimited.

———. 1976. The profession. In *Landmarks of Library Literature, 1876–1976,* ed. Dianne J. Ellsworth and Norman D. Stevens, 21–23. Metuchen, NJ: The Scarecrow Press.

Drucker, Peter F. 2001. *The Essential Drucker.* New York: HarperBusiness.

———. 2008. *Management.* Revised edition. With Joseph A. Maciariello. New York: Collins.

———. *Managing in a Time of Great Change.* New York: Truman Talley Books/Dutton.

Dunn, Paul and Ronald J. Baker. 2003. *The Firm of the Future: A Guide for Accountants, Lawyers, and Other Professional Services.* Hoboken, NJ: John Wiley & Sons.

Forrest, Charles. 2005. Segmenting the library market, reaching out to the user community by reaching across the organization.*Georgia Library Quarterly,* 42, 1, 4–7.

Glazier, Jack D. and Robert Grover. 2002. A multidisciplinary framework for theory building. In *Current theory in library and information science,* issue ed. William E. McGrath. *Library Trends* 50 No. 3, 317–329.

Gray, William S. and Ruth Monroe. 1929. *The Reading Interests and Habits of Adults.* New York: Macmillan.

Green, Samuel S. 1976. Personal relations between librarians and readers. In *Landmarks of Library Literature, 1876–1976,* ed. Dianne J. Ellsworth and Norman D. Stevens, 319–330. Metuchen, NJ: The Scarecrow Press.

Greer, Roger C. 1987. A model for the discipline of information science. In *Intellectual foundations for information professionals,* ed. Herbert K. Achleitner, 3–25. Boulder, CO: Social Science Monographs; New York: Distributed by Columbia University Press.

Greer, Roger C. and Martha L. Hale. 1982. The community analysis process. In *Public Librarianship, a Reader,* ed. Jane Robbins-Carter, 358–366. Littleton, CO.: Libraries Unlimited.

Greer, Roger C., Robert J. Grover, and Susan G. Fowler. 2007. *Introduction to the Library and Information Professions*. Westport, CT and London: Libraries Unlimited.

Hale, Martha. L. 1986. Administrators and information: a review of methodologies used for diagnosing information use. In *Advances in librarianship*, Volume 14, ed. W. Simonton, 75–99. Orlando, FL: Academic Press.

Hamel, Gary and Bill Breen. 2007. *The Future of Management*. Boston, MA: Harvard Business School Press.

Harris, Michael H. 1995. *History of Libraries in the Western World*. 4th ed. Metuchen, NJ & London: Scarecrow Press.

Kuhlthau, Carol C. 2004. *Seeking Meaning: A Process Approach to Library and Information Services*. Westport, CT: Libraries Unlimited.

LaRue, James. Libraries should measure community impact. September 3, 2009. http://www.douglascountylibraries.org/AboutUs/LaRuesViews/2009/090309 (accessed November 24, 2009).

Lerner, Frederick Andrew. 1999. *Libraries Through the Ages*. New York: Continuum.

Lincoln, Y. S. and E. G. Guba. 1985. *Naturalistic Inquiry*. Beverly Hills, CA: Sage Publications.

Mason, Robert. 2007. Culture: an overlooked key to unlocking organizational knowledge. In *Cross-cultural perspectives on knowledge management*, ed. David J. Pauleen, 21–34. Westport, CT and London: Libraries Unlimited.

Mohan-Neill, Sumaria Indra. 1995. The influence of firm's age and size on its environmental scanning activities. *Journal of Small Business Management*, 33, 4, 10–21.

Plosker, George R. 2002. Conducting user surveys: an ongoing information imperative. *Online*, 26, 5, 64–68.

Powell, Ronald R. 2004. *Basic Research Methods for Librarians*. 4th ed. Library and Information Science Text Series. Westport, CT and London: Libraries Unlimited.

Richardson, John V. 1982. *The Spirit of Inquiry: The Graduate Library School at Chicago, 1921–51*. Chicago: American Library Association.

Schneider, Georg. 1961. *Theory and History of Bibliography*. Trans. by Ralph Robert Shaw. New York: Scarecrow Press.

Sheehy, Gail. 1976. *Passages: Predictable Crises of Adult Life*. New York: Dutton.

———. 1995. *New Passages: Mapping Your Life Across Time*. New York: Random House.

Shera, Jesse Hauk. 1965. *Foundations of the Public Library: The Origins of the Public Library Movement in New England, 1629–1885*. Hamden, CT: Shoe String Press.

———. 1965. *Libraries and the Organization of Knowledge*. Hamden, CT: Archon Books.

———. 1973. *Knowing Books and Men; Knowing Computers, Too*. Littleton, CO: Libraries Unlimited.

Siatri, Rania. 1999. The evolution of user studies. *Libri*, 49, 132–141.

Tenopir, Carol. 2003. What user studies tell us. *Library Journal*, 128, 14 (September 1, 2003): 32.

Wallace, Karen. 2007. Marketing mindset: focusing on the customer, from technical services to circulation. *Feliciter*, 3, 126–129.

Waples, Douglas. n.d. *People and Print: Social Aspects of Reading in the Depression.* Chicago: The University of Chicago Press.

Waples, Douglas. 1932. The relation of subject interests to actual reading. *Library Quarterly*, 2, 1, 42–70.

Waples, Douglas, Bernard Berelson, and Franklyn R. Bradshaw. 1940. *What Reading Does to People.* Chicago: The University of Chicago Press.

Waples, Douglas and Leon Carnovsky. 1939. *Libraries and Readers in the State of New York.* Chicago: The University of Chicago Press.

Warner, E. S., A. D. Murray, and V. E. Palmour. 1973. Information needs of urban residents. U.S. Department of Health, Education and Welfare, Office of Education, Bureau of Libraries and Learning Resources. Cited in Siatri (1999, 136).

Weick, Karl E. and Kathleen M. Sutcliffe. *Managing the Unexpected: Resilient Performance in an Age of Uncertainty.* 2007. 2nd edition. San Francisco: Jossey-Bass.

Westbrook, Lynn. 2001. *Identifying and Analyzing User Needs: A complete handbook and ready-to-use assessment handbook with disk.* New York and London: Neal-Schuman Publishers.

Wiegand, Wayne A. 1996. *Irrepressible Reformer: A Biography of Melvil Dewey.* Chicago: American Library Association.

Wilson, Patrick. 1977. *Public Knowledge, Private Ignorance: Toward a Library and Information Policy.* Westport, CT and London: Greenwood Press.

Wilson, T. D. 1981. On user studies and information needs. *The Journal of Documentation*, 37, 1, 3–15.

INDEX

Page numbers followed by *f* indicate figures; and those followed by *t* indicate tables.

Achleitner, Herbert, 11
Action research, 170
Adams, Mignon S., 69
Adams County, 154–155; government, 132; population, 134
Age distribution among communities, population and, 140*t*
Agencies: collecting data on, 124–125; community analysis data, 148–151; global network of, 24; government, 91–92, 102; systematic approach to discovering, 96–97
Agencies, definition of, 95–102; examples of agencies, 97–102; identifying agencies, 97; sources of information, 96–97
Agencies, examples of, 97–102; business, 100; colleges and universities, 101–102; cultural, 99–100; educational, 100; government, 98; government agencies, 102; health care, 98–99; municipalities, 97–100; private enterprise, 102; religious, 98; schools, 101
Agencies, information needs of, 95–103; definition of agencies, 95–102; implication for library and information services, 102–103
Agencies case studies, 149–150; business, 150; cultural, 150;

educational, 150; government, 149; health care, 149; recreation, 150; religious, 149
Aguilar, Francis Joseph, 60, 61, 62
American Association of Law Libraries, 18
American Civil War, 9
American FactFinder, 80, 81
American Library Association (ALA), 10, 18, 165, 168
American Society for Information Science and Technology (ASIST), 18
Analyses: community, 63–64; implementing community, 121–136; registration file, 127–128
Analysis model, community, 45*f*
Archival function. *See* Bibliographic/ archival function
Assertive level of service, 17
Assertive service, 174

Baldwinsville: study, 46; system, 44
Barnard, Henry, 166
Beck, Jeffrey A., 69
Bedroom suburbs, 153
Behavioral processes of, 77–78
Bibliographic/archival function, 164–165
Bibliographic instruction, 167
Bopp, Richard E., 171

Boston Public Library, 8
Bourgeois, L. J., III, 61
Brighton, possible information services
    for, 177–178*t*
Brighton Sentinel Blade online
    newspaper, 145
Brighton's residents, place of work for, 154*t*
Brighton's workforce, residence for, 153*t*
Business, 100
Business case studies, 150
Business environment, today's, 181–186;
    implementing system for change,
    184–186; leading change, 183–184
Butler, Pierce, 175

CARI (Community Analysis Research
    Institute), 39
CARI model, component parts of, 47–48
Carnovsky, Leon, 57
Case studies: agencies, 149–150;
    community analysis data, 138–141;
    implementing community analysis,
    131–135; introduction to Rangeview
    Library District (RLD), 132; lifestyles,
    151–154; map, 155–157; registration
    file, 157; shelf list data, 157–159;
    workshop, 132–135
Census Bureau, U.S., 80
Census data, 80–82
Census Products Catalog, 82
Centre for Research on User Studies at
    Sheffield University, 59
Change: implementing system for,
    184–186; leading, 183–184;
    managing, 2–3
Civil War, American, 9
Cleveland, Harlan, 21
Clientele, knowing, 3–4
Climate, 110–111; elements of
    community's, 110–111; information
    about community's, 111
Clinton, DeWitt, 8, 166
Coalition for Networked Information
    (CNI), 19
Colleges: example of agencies, 101–102;
    example of groups, 90–91; number
    analysis, 130–131
Collins, Jim, 186, 187
Columbia University libraries, 9, 10,
    166, 171
Columbia University reference
    department, 170

Communication, 113–115; information
    about, 115; technology influences on,
    114–115
Communication patterns, identifying
    community, 113–114
Communication patterns among people,
    interaction and, 26
Communities: educational attainment for
    six, 141*t*; effective analysis of, 50–51;
    population and age distribution among,
    140*t*; racial trends in six, 141*t*; sources
    of information about customs in, 109
Community, exploring culture in, 106–119;
    climate, 110–111; communication,
    113–115; community-ness, 115–117;
    customs, 109; economic life, 117–118;
    history, 107–108; leisure activities,
    111–112; social issues, 118–119; topo-
    graphical features, 109–110; transporta-
    tion and traffic patterns, 112–113;
    values, 108–109
Community, identifying groups in, 85–92;
    examples of groups, 88–92; sources of
    information, 87–88
Community analysis, 63–64, 123–129;
    collecting data on individuals, groups,
    agencies, and lifestyles, 123–129;
    library resource analysis, 126–129
Community analysis, definition of, 43–48;
    component parts of CARI model, 47–
    48; evolution of Greer community
    analysis model, 44–47
Community analysis, implementing,
    121–136; case studies, 131–135;
    community analysis, 123–129;
    meaning of numbers, 129–131;
    organizing to gather data, 121–123
Community analysis, theoretical
    framework for, 39–56; adapting to
    community change, 48–51; definition of
    community analysis, 43–48; role of
    information professional, 39–43; science
    of information professions, 51–55
Community analysis data, 123–126;
    agencies, 124–125; groups, 124;
    individuals, 123–124; lifestyles,
    125–126
Community analysis data, extrapolating
    meaning from, 137–161; agencies,
    148–151; groups, 142–148;
    individuals, 137–142; lifestyles, 151–
    155; map case study, 155–157;

registration file case study, 157; review of community analysis process, 159–160; shelf list data case study, 157–159; what data tells us, 137
Community analysis model, 45f
Community analysis model, evolution of Greer, 44–47
Community analysis process, review of, 159–160
Community Analysis Research Institute (CARI), 5
Community change, adapting to, 48–51; community change requires understanding past and present, 49–50; effective analysis of community, 50–51; social science theories, 50–51
Community change requires understanding past and present, 49–50
Community information, using Internet to gather, 72
Community information and knowledge infrastructure, 23–30; community knowledge infrastructure, 28–30; social knowledge and information services, 27–28
Community information-needs analysis (CINA), 63
Community knowledge infrastructure, 28–30
Community knowledge system, 25–26; interaction and communication patterns among people, 26; knowledge generated by society, 25–26; practical skills or tools, 26; values adopted by group of people, 26
Community-ness, 115–117; elements of, 116; information about, 116–117
Community's climate: elements of, 110–111; sources of information about, 111
Community's customs, elements of, 109
Community's values: elements of, 108; sources of information about, 108–109
Contribution, 185
Costa, Jorge, 62
Councils, market, 65
Cultural, agencies, 99–100
Cultural case studies, 150
Cultural function, 167–169
Culture, 31–32
Culture in community, 106–119; climate, 110–111; communication, 113–115; community-ness, 115–117; customs,

109; economic life, 117–118; history, 107–108; leisure activities, 111–112; social issues, 118–119; topographical features, 109–110; transportation and traffic patterns, 112–113; values, 108–109
Customers: retaining, 186; why they leave companies, 186
Customs, 109; elements of community's, 109; information about community's, 109
Cycle, diagnostic, 42f
Cycle, service, 39–41; diagnosis, 40; evaluation, 41; implementation, 40–41; prescription, 40; treatment, 40–41

Data: applying to service scenarios, 175–179; community analysis, 137–161; gathering for decision-making, 57–74; registration, 72
Data, locating for individuals, 79–82; census data, 80–82; library registration files, 79–80; using Internet, 82
Data, organizing to gather, 121–123; organizing into teams, 122–123; whom to involve, 122
Data case study, shelf list, 157–159
Data collection on individuals, 143–144t
Data-gathering: methods, 67f; systematic, 68
Data meaning for library services, 142
Decision-making, gathering data for, 57–74; reader studies, 57–58; studies of information needs, 58–68; using and not using surveys, 69–71; using Internet to gather community information, 72; using registration data, 72
D'Elia, George, 58
Denver Regional Council of Governments (DRCOG), 154
Department of Education, US, 46
Dewey, Melvil, 4, 9, 10, 12, 58, 165, 166, 168
Diagnosis process, 40f
Diagnostic cycle, 42f
Diagnostic process in information services, 41–43
Douglas County Colorado libraries, 182
Drucker, Peter, 2, 183, 184

Economic life, 117–118
Economic system, 33–34

Economic trends: identifying community's, 117; information about community's, 117–118
Economy, library, 10, 166
Education, 139–141
Education, US Department of, 46
Educational, agencies, 100
Educational attainment for six communities, 141t
Educational case studies, 150
Educational function, 166–167
Emporia State University, 11
Emporia State University School of Library and Information Management, 135, 138
Enterprise, private, 91–92, 102
Environmental context for information psychology, 79
Environmental scanning, 60–63
Environmental scanning, systematic approach to, 62–63

FedStats, 82
File analysis, registration, 127–128
Files, library registration, 79–80
Focus groups, 71
Forrest, Charles, 65
Fowler, Susan G., 7, 12, 51, 132–133, 164
Freas, Lynda, 155, 159, 160
Functions: bibliographic/archival, 164–165; cultural, 167–169; educational, 166–167; information, 170–172, 174t; of information and library services, 164–173; recreational, 172–173; research, 169–170

Geography, physical, 32
Global information infrastructure, 12–16; library information professionals in information infrastructure, 13–16
Global network of people, organizations, agencies, policies, processes, and technologies, 24
Government, 98; agencies, 91–92, 102; case studies, 149
Gray, William S., 57
Green, Samuel Swett, 9, 170, 171
Greer, Roger C., 11, 17, 23, 29, 43, 51, 63, 85, 132–133
Greer community analysis model, evolution of, 44–47
Group information, summary of, 93f

Group matrix, 88f
Groups: collecting data on, 124; community analysis data, 142–148; focus, 71
Groups, examples of, 88–92; colleges, 90–91; government agencies, 91–92; municipalities, 89; private enterprise, 91–92; schools, 90; universities, 90–91
Groups, identifying in community, 85–92; examples of groups, 88–92; sources of information, 87–88
Groups, information needs of, 85–93; identifying groups in community, 85–92; implications for library and information services, 92–93; what one wants to know, 92
Grover, Robert J., 7, 11, 12, 51, 132–133, 164
Guidelines for Information Service, 171

Hale, Martha L., 17, 43, 63, 67, 68, 85
Hard sciences, 51
Harvard Business Review (HBR), 186
Health care, 98–99
Health care case studies, 149
High reliability organizations (HROs), 185
Historical information and communities, 107–108
History: elements of community's, 107; exploring culture in community, 107–108; of library services, 7–12
Household: value, 152t; vehicles available per, 152t
Housing occupancy, 152t

Implementation, issues in, 181–187; challenge ahead, 186–187; retaining customers, 186; today's business environment, 181–186
Impressions, 67
Individual knowledge, 22
Individuals: community analysis data, 137–142; data collection on, 123–124, 143–144t; definition of, 75–77
Individuals, community analysis data: case study results, 138–141; data meaning for library services, 142; education, 139–141; population, 139; racial trends, 141
Individuals, information needs of, 75–83; information psychology, 77–79; locating data for individuals, 79–82

Individuals, locating data for, 79–82; census data, 80–82; library registration files, 79–80; using Internet, 82

Information: community, 23–30; defined, 21; functions, 170–172, 174*t*; literacy, 36, 167; sociology of, 53–55; summary of group, 93*f*; use studies, 64–65; using Internet to gather community, 72

Information and knowledge, six functions of, 29

Information and library services, functions of, 164–173; bibliographic/ archival function, 164–165; cultural function, 167–169; educational function, 166–167; information function, 170–172; recreational function, 172–173; research function, 169–170

Information and library services functions summary, 173

Information infrastructure, global, 12–16; library information professionals in information infrastructure, 13–16

Information needs, assessing, 35–37

Information needs, studies of, 58–68; environmental scanning, 60–63; qualitative research methods and intuition, 65–68

Information needs of agencies, 95–103; definition of agencies, 95–102; implication for library and information services, 102–103

Information needs of groups, 85–93; identifying groups in community, 85–92; implications for library and information services, 92–93; what one wants to know, 92

Information needs of individuals, 75–83; information psychology, 77–79; locating data for individuals, 79–82

Information policy, 34

Information professional, role of, 39–43; diagnostic process in information services, 41–43

Information professions, science of, 51–55; information psychology, 52–53; sociology of information, 53–55

Information psychology, 52–53, 77–79; behavioral processes of, 77–78; environmental context for, 79; theory supporting, 78

Information resources and knowledge systems, 30–31

Information science, 51

Information services: for Brighton, 177–178*t*; customizing, 35–37; diagnostic process in, 41–43; model for assessing, 36*f*; social knowledge and, 27–28

Information services, conceptualizing, 163–174; functions of information and library services, 164–173

Information services, implications for, 16–19, 150–151; influence of technology on information services, 17–19; levels of user-centered services, 17

Information services, implications for library and, 92–93, 102–103

Information services, influence of technology on, 17–19; challenges of keeping current with technology, 18–19

Information services, planning, 163–180; conceptualizing information services, 163–174; role of professional, 175–179

Information sources by managers, 61–62

Information Studies, Syracuse University School of, 46

Information transfer, 26

Information transfer cycle, 14*f*

Infrastructure: community knowledge, 28–30; global information, 12–16; knowledge, 23–30, 29*f*

Instruction, bibliographic, 167

Interaction and communication patterns among people, 26

Internet, 72, 82

Interviews, 70

Introduction to the Library and Information Professions (Greer, Grover, and Fowler), 132–133

Intuition, qualitative research methods and, 65–68; impressions, 67; scientific research, 68; systematic data-gathering, 68; use of intuition, 66–67

Jones, Chandra, 155

Knowledge: defined, 21; generated by society, 25–26; individual, 22; personal, 22; social, 22, 27–28; in society, 27*f*

Knowledge, six functions of information and, 29

Knowledge infrastructure, community information and, 23–30; community knowledge infrastructure, 28–30; social knowledge and information services, 27–28

Knowledge management (KM) literature, 22

Knowledge society, 2

Knowledge systems: information resources and, 30–31; interface of formal and informal, 31–34

Knowledge systems, community, 25–26; interaction and communication patterns among people, 26; knowledge generated by society, 25–26; practical skills or tools, 26; values adopted by group of people, 26

Knowledge systems, interface of formal and informal: culture, 31–32; economic system, 33–34; information policy, 34; legislation and regulations, 33; physical geography, 32; political structure, 32; technology, 34

Knowledge systems in society, 21–37; assessing information needs, 35–37; community information and knowledge infrastructure, 23–30; customizing information services, 35–37; definitions, 21–23; formal and informal knowledge systems and resources, 30–34

Knowledge transfer, 26

Kuhlthau, Carol C., 43

Landmarks of Tomorrow, The (Drucker), 2

LaRue, James, 182

Legislation and regulations, 33

Leisure activities: exploring culture in community, 111–112; identifying, 111–112; information about community's, 112

Levels of service, 173–174, 174t; assertive service, 174; passive service, 173; reactive service, 173–174

Libraries: Boston Public, 8; Columbia University, 9, 10, 166, 171; Douglas County Colorado, 182; in New York state school districts, 8; special, 9, 131

Libraries in society, 7–20; current changes in society, 16–19; global information infrastructure, 12–16; history of library

services, 7–12; implications for information services, 16–19; past and present, 7–20

Library and information services, implications for, 92–93, 102–103

Library economy, 10, 166

Library information professionals in information infrastructure, 13–16

Library registration files, 79–80

Library resource analysis, 126–129; map study, 126–127; registration file analysis, 127–128; shelf list study, 128–129

Library services, evolution of, 8–9

Library services, functions of information and, 164–173; bibliographic/archival function, 164–165; cultural function, 167–169; educational function, 166–167; information function, 170–172; recreational function, 172–173; research function, 169–170

Library services, history of, 7–12; emergence of new service paradigm, 9–12; evolution of library services, 8–9

Library services data, 142

Library services functions summary, information and, 173

Lifestyles, 105–120; case studies, 151–154; collecting data on, 125–126; community analysis data and, 151–155; definition of, 105–106; exploring culture in community, 106–119; summary, 154–155

Lincoln, President Abraham, 169

Literacy, information, 36, 167

Literature, knowledge management (KM), 22

Managers, information sources by, 61–62

Mann, Horace, 166

Map, case study, 155–157

Map study, 126–127

Market councils, 65

Mason, Robert, 22

Massachusetts, public libraries in, 167

Master of Library Science (MLS) degree, 10, 13

Matrix, group, 88f

Media centers, school library, 130

Medical Library Association, 18

MLS. *See* Master of Library Science (MLS) degree

Mohan-Neill, Sumaria Indra, 62
Monroe, Ruth, 57
Monthly costs, mortgage status and, 153*t*
Mortgage status and monthly costs, 153*t*
Municipalities, 89, 97–100

New Passages (Sheehy), 80
Newspaper, Brighton Sentinel Blade online, 145
New York State Development Corporation, 44
New York state school districts, libraries in, 8
Number analysis: colleges, 130–131; public libraries, 129; school library media centers, 130; special libraries, 131; universities and colleges, 130–131

OCLC, 182
O'Connor, Dan, 44
Online newspaper, Brighton Sentinel Blade, 145
Onondaga Hill Public Library, 46
Organizations, global network of, 24

Passages (Sheehy), 80
Passive level of service, 17
Passive service, 173
People: global network of, 24; interaction and communication patterns among, 26; values adopted by group of, 26
Performance, 185
Personal knowledge, 22
Physical geography, 32
Plosker, George R., 64
Policies, global network of, 24
Political, economic, social, and technological (PEST) analysis, 62
Political structure, 32
Population, 139
Population and age distribution among communities, 140*t*
Powell, Ronald R., 69, 70, 71, 127
Practical skills or tools, 26
Private enterprise, 91–92, 102
Processes, global network of, 24
Professional level of service, 43
Professionals: information, 39–43; roles of, 175–179
Professionals in information infrastructure, library information, 13–16

Professions, science of information, 51–55; information psychology, 52–53; sociology of information, 53–55
Psychology, information, 52–53, 77–79
Public libraries: Boston, 8; in Massachusetts, 167; number analysis, 129; Onondaga Hill, 46; St. Paul (Minnesota), 58

Qualitative research methods and intuition, 65–68; impressions, 67; scientific research, 68; systematic data-gathering, 68; use of intuition, 66–67
Questionnaires, written, 69–70

Racial trends, 141
Racial trends in six communities, 141*t*
Radiofrequency Identification (RFID) chip, 157
Rangeview Library District (RLD), 122, 132, 138
Reactive level of service, 17
Reactive service, 173–174
Reader studies, 57–58
Recreational function, 172–173
Recreation case studies, 150
Reference and User Services Association (RUSA), 171
Reference service, 171
Registration data, 72
Registration files: analysis, 127–128; case studies, 157; library, 79–80
Regulations, legislation and, 33
Relationship of information resources and knowledge systems, 29*f*
Religious case studies, 149
Religious service groups, 98
Research: action, 170; function, 169–170; scientific, 68
Research methods and intuition, qualitative, 65–68; impressions, 67; scientific research, 68; systematic data-gathering, 68; use of intuition, 66–67
Residence for Brighton's workforce, 153*t*
Residents: commuting to work, 154*t*; place of work for Brighton's, 154*t*
Resources, information, 30–31
Rockefeller Corporation study, 186
Rodger, Eleanor Jo, 58

Scanning, environmental, 60–63
Schneider, Georg, 44

School districts, libraries in New York state, 8
School library media centers, 130
School of Library and Information Management, Emporia State University, 135, 138
School of Library Science at Syracuse University, 11
Schools, 90, 101
Science: information, 51; of information professions, 51–55
Sciences, hard, 51
Scientific research, 68
Service, levels of, 173–174, 174*t*; assertive service, 174; passive service, 173; reactive service, 173–174
Service cycle, 39–41; diagnosis, 40; evaluation, 41; implementation, 40–41; prescription, 40; treatment, 40–41
Service paradigm, emergence of new, 9–12
Services: assertive, 174; assertive level of, 17; functions of information and library, 164–173; implications for information, 16–19, 150–151; implications for library and information, 92–93, 102–103; information, 27–28; levels of user-centered, 17; passive, 173; passive level of, 17; planning information, 163–180; professional level of, 43; reactive, 173–174; reactive level of, 17; reference, 171; technician level of, 42
Services, history of library, 7–12; emergence of new service paradigm, 9–12; evolution of library services, 8–9
Service scenarios, applying data to, 175–179
Sheehy, Gail, 80
Shelf lists: data case studies, 157–159; studies, 128–129
Shera, Jesse, 44
Siatri, Rania, 59
Skills or tools, practical, 26
Smith, Linda K., 171
Social issues: exploring culture in community, 118–119; identifying in community, 118–119; information about community, 119
Social knowledge, 22
Social knowledge and information services, 27–28
Social science theories, 50–51

Society: knowledge, 2; knowledge generated by, 25–26; knowledge in, 27*f*
Society, knowledge systems in, 21–37; assessing information needs, 35–37; community information and knowledge infrastructure, 23–30; customizing information services, 35–37; definitions, 21–23; formal and informal knowledge systems and resources, 30–34
Society, libraries in, 7–20; current changes in society, 16–19; global information infrastructure, 12–16; history of library services, 7–12; implications for information services, 16–19; past and present, 7–20
Society of American Archivists, 18
Sociology of information, 53–55
Software, Zoomerang, 69
Special libraries, 9, 131
Special Libraries Association (SLA), 18, 169
State and County QuickFacts, 81
State and Metropolitan Area Data Book, 81
Statistical Abstract of the United States, 81
St. Paul (Minnesota) Public Library, 58
Strategic Information Scanning System (SISS), 62–63
Studies: information use, 64–65; Rockefeller Corporation, 186; shelf list, 128–129
Suburbs, bedroom, 153
Surveys, using and not using, 69–71; focus groups, 71; interviews, 70; when not to use, 71; written questionnaires, 69–70
Sutcliffe, Kathleen M., 185
Syracuse University: School of Information Studies, 46; School of Library Science at, 11; US Department of Education at, 46
Systematic data-gathering, 68

Teams, organizing into, 122–123
Technician level of service, 42
Technologies, global network of, 24
Technology, 34; challenges of keeping current with, 18–19; influences on communication, 114–115
Technology on information services, influence of, 17–19
Tenopir, Carol, 64
Theories, social science, 50–51
Today's business environment, 181–186

Tools, practical skills or, 26
Topographical features: elements of, 109–110; information about community's, 110
Traffic patterns: sources of information about community, 113; transportation and, 112–113
Transfer: information, 26; knowledge, 26
Transportation and traffic patterns, 112–113

Universities and colleges: examples of agencies, 101–102; identifying groups in communities, 90–91; number analysis, 130–131
U.S. Census Bureau, 80
US Department of Education at Syracuse University, 46
User-centered services, levels of, 17
User needs, assessment of customization to meet, 36f
Users, changing needs of, 64

Values: adopted by group of people, 26; elements of community's, 108; household, 152t; information about community's, 108–109
Vehicles available per household, 152t

Wallace, Karen, 60
Waples, Douglas, 57
Weick, Karl E., 185
Westbrook, Lynn, 63
Wilson, Patrick, 22
Wilson, T. D., 58
Work, residents commuting to, 154t
Work for Brighton's residents, place of, 154t
Workforce, residence for Brighton's, 153t
Workshop case studies, 132–135
Written questionnaires, 69–70

Zoomerang software, 69

About the Authors

ROBERT J. GROVER is retired Associate Vice President for Academic Affairs at Emporia State University and former Dean and Professor in the School of Library and Information Management. His Ph.D. in Library and Information Science is from Indiana University. He co-edited *The Handy Five; Planning and Assessing Integrated Information Skills Instruction* (2001) and co-authored *Introduction to the Library and Information Professions* (2007). His awards include Association for Library and Information Science Education Outstanding Teaching Award, Beta Phi Mu International Library and Information Science Honorary Society, Pi Lambda Theta Education Honorary Society, Phi Kappa Phi, and Phi Eta Sigma.

ROGER C. GREER is Dean Emeritus of the School of Library and Information Management, University of Southern California, former dean and professor at Syracuse University, and Professor Emeritus at Emporia State University. His Ph.D. in Library and Information Science was earned at Rutgers University. He recently co-authored with Robert Grover and Susan Fowler *Introduction to the Library and Information Professions*. He has conducted more than 120 workshops on community analysis. Among his awards are Rutgers University School of Communication, Information and Library Science Alumnus of the Year Award (1987), and Emporia State University Roe Cross Distinguished Professor.

JOHN AGADA is currently Director of the Department of Library, Information and Media Studies (LIMS), Chicago State University. Previously, he was on the faculties at Ahmadu Bello University, Nigeria, University of Wisconsin-Milwaukee, and Emporia State University. He earned his BLS and M.Ed. (Curriculum & Instruction) from Ahmadu Bello University and Ph.D. from the University of Pittsburgh. Dr. Agada's research has focused on psychology of information use and attributes of library and information professionals. An accomplished scholar with numerous publications to his credit, Dr. Agada has also designed and managed several grant-funded projects on community analysis and information services design for underserved populations, and the education of minority and international LIS professionals. A frequent visitor to Africa, where he consults for several LIS institutions and organizations, Dr. Agada and his family reside in Chicago, Illinois